When God Intervenes, LET HIM

AMY SIMMONS ALFORD

Amazing Faith
PUBLISHING

Amazing Faith
PUBLISHING

Published by Amazing Faith Publishers
ISBN: 978-0-578-07019-3 (paperback)
ISBN: 978-0-578-07018-6 (hardcover)

Have you ever wondered if God hears your prayers? Or, maybe you believe that He hears them, but you assume that He chooses to ignore some and answer others. This book is real-life testimony that God not only hears your prayers, but He answers every one of them. It is a fast-paced journey through Amy's life, as she vividly recalls the countless times God has intervened and answered her prayers. You will be caught up in the sometimes heart-pounding, sometimes miraculous, but always heart-warming ways in which God has met Amy in her time of need, and provided wisdom and guidance to navigate her through the crisis. In every occasion, Amy has known an inner peace that wasn't shaken by the circumstance or catastrophe. I recommend this book for all who yearn to have that same kind of relationship with God.

Gayle D. Beebe, Ph.D. | President, Westmont College

Through her very personal and fascinating life experiences, Amy beautifully illustrates that *when God intervenes– let Him!* I really enjoyed her book and learned so much about her and her relationship with the Lord. Letting God intervene in her life's journey makes her the SAME KIND OF DIFFERENT AS ME!

Ron Hall | Author of *Same Kind of Different As Me*

This book will keep you on the edge of your seat as Amy describes in detail her incredible life stories. Amy puts her faith into action through the power of prayer, and we as readers are *not* left wondering how to find meaning and fulfillment through a relationship with God.

Joy Weaver | Speaker & author of *Socially Savvy*

When God intervenes in your life, where do you run? This powerful book shows from personal experiences how to really let go and let God. Amy has spoken, and I am listening for this freedom we have in God to let Him have His way.

Thelma Wells, M.Min., D.D. (Hon.) | Speaker & author; President, A Woman of God Ministries

When God Intervenes gives an intimate glimpse inside Amy's daily walk with Christ. Full of heartwarming stories of family and friends, Amy takes you on a journey that testifies to God's faithfulness and love for his children. This will encourage your heart and reaffirm your heart for our loving Creator.

Joe White | President, Kanakuk Kamps; Nationally renowned speaker & author

Amy is amazing. She has such an honest and generous way of sharing her stories and lessons. Sometimes she makes you laugh, and other times she makes you cry…but she always makes you feel better. Her writing style is so natural that you don't realize you are being taught. I think she learned that from Sandy! Her books are a blessing to anyone who reads them, and her passion for God and His Word is contagious.

Kimberly Schlegel Whitman | Founder, RSVPcalendar.com. Author, speaker, and lifestyle expert on DFW's #1 Morning Show

Reading this book made me so teary-eyed. I was riveted by the detailed description and recall of such valuable and powerful events. Anyone who reads this book will be inspired to run to their loved ones...to just appreciate and give thanks for their love. I will share this beautiful collection of stories with everyone I come in contact with! It is such a beautiful reminder how God answers our prayers every day.

Sheree J. Wilson | Film and television actress, featured in *Dallas* and *Walker Texas Ranger*

Also by Amy Simmons Alford
When God Has a Way, No Other Way Works

For my three parents: Mom, Harold, and Dad (who watches from above). All of you raised me in Christian homes and taught me values and morals that shaped my life. Thank you for your encouragement, support, and love throughout my years, especially the rebellious ones. You have been beside me every step of the way, always with encouraging words. Your amazing love and strength has encouraged me. I love you with all my heart.

I want to thank all of you who helped me write and encouraged me to finish this book. The creative team at Fluency spent countless hours skillfully shaping this book to its final form. Joy Weaver, who acted as my "author role model" and soundboard, helped me in many ways—thank you! And for all of you who actually played a part in one or more stories, I'm so glad God protected us and watched over us so we can read this and see how He really did intervene! Most of all, I want to thank my Lord and Savior, Jesus Christ, for being so patient with me when I strayed and for waiting for me when I decided to turn back to Him. May this book glorify You and what You have done in my life.

TABLE OF CONTENTS

ABOUT THE AUTHOR

NATIONALLY RENOWNED AUTHOR, SPEAKER, AND photographer Amy Simmons Alford has photographed some of the world's most powerful and respected leaders, including President George W. Bush and his wife Laura, former President George H.W. Bush, Oprah Winfrey, Benjamin Netanyahu, Senator Kay Bailey Hutchinson, and Chuck Norris. However, nothing excites her more than capturing the special moments of children and families in a relaxed, outdoor setting. She graduated from Brooks Institute of Photography, one of the most prestigious colleges for photography in the country.

She loves to travel throughout the world. However, her favorite places include her family farms in Ozark, Arkansas and McKinney, Texas; summers in Aspen, Colorado; and vacationing in Santa Barbara, California. When she is not behind the camera or at her desk writing, she loves adventurous activities like snow skiing, four wheelers, paragliding, and hiking. On the softer side, a beautiful sunset, thunderstorms, and a good fire are at the top of Amy's list of favorites.

Her first book, *When God Has A Way, No Other Way Works,* opened many doors for her to speak and encourage others in their journey. Since her first public speaking engagement at the White House, Amy has spoken at retreats and special events around the country. You may have heard Amy in various radio interviews or even seen her on television shows such as *Daily Talk.*

Showing people there is someone who cares, especially in their time of need, is important to her. Reaching out to people is one of Amy's spiritual gifts, and she supports several charities including Kids Across America and East West Ministries. Amy feels strongly about sponsoring short-term mission trips, following Christ's command to "Go into all nations and spread the Gospel." She also volunteers at her church in the prayer ministry.

Her second book, *When God Intervenes, Let Him,* is a collection of personal experiences when God intervened in her life in special and amazing ways. It shows how God will intervene when you trust Him and are available to Him. She believes everything happens for a reason and is convinced that God has specific plans and purposes for every situation that happens in our lives. She will challenge you to make an investment in a relationship with God so you, too, will agree: When God Intervenes, Let Him!

She resides in Dallas, Texas.

INTRODUCTION

Y MENTOR AND ADOPTED GRANDMOTHER, SANDY, and I used to joke when I told her I wrote my first book about the impact her walk with the Lord and her teachings had on me. She humbly said, "Well, just order a copy for me and one for you and maybe one or two more" (thinking nobody but us would want to read it). We laughed about that until the day *When God Has a Way, No Other Way Works* had sold close to 4000 copies!

We never dreamed the impact our first book would have. The lives it touched, the relationships that were cultivated—God did it all. As you will see in some of the stories in this second book, He had a bigger plan for what He inspired me to write. Every time I put pen to paper to write, I ask the Lord to put His words on the page and to block my way if I try to write something He does not want me to write.

I believe everything happens for a reason. When I endure a trial in my life or I experience a "God thing," I know it's Him working His plan through me. Over the years, I have developed a close and intimate relationship with Christ, and I have experienced things I never knew were possible. Although now I realize that nothing is impossible with God (Luke 1:37)!

At the same time, I also know that I don't have all the answers. But I don't feel I need to know them, because my faith in Christ sustains me in every situation. He has proven His presence, existence, love, mercy, grace, and forgiveness so many times. That's why I don't ask, "Why, Lord?" anymore. Now, when I'm faced with a challenge, I just say, "Help me through this. Guide me, show me what You want me to learn, and thank You, Lord." I don't always understand why God does things. Sometimes I can see why He did something a certain way, but sometimes not. I just know in my heart there is a reason and purpose for everything, so I put my trust and faith in the One who knows, and I go with it!

In this book, I once again use my trials and experiences to relate God's work and His Word to you. I wanted to write these true short stories as evidence for the existence of a loving God so people could relate to what God teaches us through His Word. What has happened in my life proves to me that God exists—and it proves that He loves me and cares for me. He hears our prayers and cries for help. No matter the outcome, He is in control. Therefore, I have total faith that His ways and plans are the best for my life!

For you, the reader, some stories will provide stronger evidence than others that God exists. But for me, all of these stories are evidence that God is real, and He listens to those who love Him. When you develop a love relationship with God (and I hope that you will, or you already have), you will also start seeing how He is working in your life—and you'll have your own stories to share.

*"Come and listen, all you who fear God, and I
will tell you what he did for me.
For I cried out to him for help, praising him as I
spoke…He paid attention to my prayer.
Praise God, who did not ignore my prayer
or withdraw his unfailing love from me."*

Psalm 66:16-17, 19-20 NKJ

When God Intervenes in FAMILY

A TALE OF TWO KIDNEYS

M Y MOM MARRIED A MAN NAMED HAROLD ON JUNE 14, 1980. I am so happy she married someone who loves and adores her and treats her like a queen. They have a very loving and tender marriage. Out of the 30 years they have been married, they have only been apart three nights! Mom is a loving, kind, tender-hearted, and giving woman who loves her family and the Lord. She was a beauty queen at SMU (Southern Methodist University) and still remains as beautiful today (if not more) as she was in college.

Harold was from a small town (population 150) and ended up doing quite well for himself in the business world. To say he is intelligent is an understatement. In my opinion, he is brilliant, and his mind works at a capacity very few people can grasp. He is honest, kind, overly generous, loving, and tender. Both Mom and Harold have taken good care of themselves, and for that I am thankful. Over the years, Harold and I have developed a wonderful, loving relationship. I am so blessed to have parents who love me and care for me the way they do. Some "stepparent" situations are difficult, but I am so blessed to have a stepdad who truly loves and cares for me. Thirty years ago, I had no idea what would be happening in our lives when Mom remarried, but God did. He knew when my mom married Harold what was in store for us as a family, especially in early 2008.

In December of 2007, my mom called me, as she usually does each morning to ask about my day. After I reeled off the day's activities, she casually said, "Honey, Harold has not been feeling well, and we had some tests done. Both of his kidneys are failing, and he needs a kidney transplant."

I was in shock. I remember looking at my dazed reaction in the reflection of my bathroom mirror. I swallowed and said, "Well, where do we get one?"

"We have to find someone to donate."

"Mom, I can do it," I said. "I am the youngest and healthiest, and I can bounce back quicker than anyone."

"Oh, Honey, I couldn't bear to have you and Harold in the hospital at the same time. I'll be talking to the doctors today. I'll get more information and see what we need to do."

I hung up the phone and immediately put together a group of 40 people on an email prayer list. These were people I knew I could count on to pray. I asked them to please pray for the perfect donor for Harold since he needed the surgery fairly quickly. His kidneys were only functioning at about five percent. Soon, over 15 volunteers of close friends, family, and employees were offering their kidney for Harold. My brother, Andy, and I were tested and discovered we were both the same blood type as Harold. However, Mom put us on hold because she didn't want to have her husband and child in surgery at the same time—not for something this serious.

Meanwhile, the other possible donors were being

cut from the list each week. Our concern grew as the surgery date came closer with no firm plans. Harold was deteriorating rapidly. He lost so much weight and looked severely weak and thin. Several times, I had to hide my tears so he wouldn't see. It was killing me and Mom to see him declining so quickly.

I remember one day Harold had been in the hospital for two or three nights having tests done. The phone rang in his room. Mom was there with him and heard him say, "Hello? Hi George...Well, not too good...I have to have a kidney transplant...okay, thank you." And he hung up.

Mom said, "Who was that?"

"George W. Bush," Harold said nonchalantly and picked up his water bottle to take a sip.

"You're kidding! The President? How did he know?" my mom inquired.

"He knows everything," he said with his dry sense of humor.

President Bush had heard from someone that Harold was not doing well. Harold and President Bush had met years ago, and they see each other from time to time. Before the President was governor, he lived three blocks from us when I was growing up. Somehow, he found out where Harold was and called his hospital room. Can you imagine being the hospital receptionist for that call?

I'm not good at handling situations where family members are hurting. I tend to become very emotional and stressed out. About six weeks before Harold's surgery, I began to have a strong pain in my left arm. It was shooting down my shoulder and into my hand, and

I was in constant pain for two weeks. However, I didn't want to burden anyone with my aches and pains in light of everything else going on, so I stayed silent.

One night at dinner, I decided to casually mention the pain. Mom put down her fork and said, "What? Pain in your left arm? You know what that means…heart attack! Honey, please don't have a heart attack! Let's get through the kidney transplant first!"

She said it jokingly and we all giggled, knowing she was kidding. I went home that night, got ready for bed and began flipping pages in my Bible. My friend, Laulie, had emailed a verse for me to read earlier that day, so I looked it up. It read, "Have mercy on me, O God, have mercy on me, for in you my soul takes refuge. I will take refuge in the shadow of your wings until the disaster has passed" Psalm 57:1. Wow. That verse came at the perfect time. I laid the Bible on my chest and thought, "Did God write that for me or what?"

I began to pray aloud, "Lord, I need You to replace my stress and fear with Your peace and comfort. Please remove the pain in my arm. I don't know what is going on with it, but I'm asking You to remove the pain." My next request I had not even thought about saying; it just came out unexpectedly. "…And Lord, if You want me to be the donor, then I want to be in Your will. If I'm the one, then give me a peace about it. All I want is for You to use me for Your purpose." By the time I finished praying, tears were streaming down my face. I also felt as if a ton of weight had been lifted from my shoulders because I had just turned my fears, worries, and stress over to Him. I think I fell asleep with a smile on my face.

The next morning, I spent some time in my "prayer" chair, a comfortable wingback chair in front of the fireplace in my bedroom. That is where I have quiet time in the mornings, my time alone with God. I pray for family, friends, others, myself, our soldiers, our country, and much more. I also read Scripture and a devotional from *Jesus Calling*, by Sarah Young. (Each day applies to my life. I highly recommend reading it!) If I have time, I will read from another daily devotional book called *Experiencing God Day by Day*. I highly recommend everyone getting that book, too. A devotional takes five minutes or less to read, and it is a great way to start your day. After a few minutes of sitting in my prayer chair, I noticed the pain in my left arm was gone. No pain whatsoever. Gone, just like that.

> "Lord, I need You to replace my stress and fear with Your peace and comfort."

Almost at the same time, I felt something else—something I've felt before but couldn't identify for a few seconds. Then it hit me: *peace*. I felt it pour over me as if someone had draped a blanket around my shoulders and held me close. It was a feeling I can't explain, but if you have experienced it, you know what I mean.

I sat there and physically felt the Holy Spirit in the room, as if He were holding me. I even looked around the room thinking someone had opened a door. However, the bedroom door was closed. It was a wonderful, peaceful, calming feeling. One thought came to my mind: "I'm going to be the donor." That thought went through my mind over and over, and I had this incredible sense of contentment. It was as if God was letting me know, "You are going to be the donor, and I'm covering you in peace, just as you asked." This feeling lasted about 20 minutes. During that time, I picked up the phone to call my mom. (In our house, if the phone rings before eight in the morning or after ten at night, we know something is wrong.) It was about 7:45 that morning when I called.

"Mom?"

"What?" she said breathlessly. (Her mother's instinct told her something was up.)

"I think I'm going to be the donor," I whispered, as if I might run off the Holy Spirit if I spoke up louder.

"What? Why? What makes you think that?"

"I can feel this great sense of peace. It's in the room with me. I'm supposed to be the donor!"

Mom wasn't convinced. "I don't feel the peace. Give me some of *your* peace," she suggested.

From that day on, I knew in the back of my mind I would be the donor, although we did not act on it right away. We were four weeks away from the surgery, but I went ahead and claimed several scriptures that would help me prepare. I claimed Isaiah 41:10, 13, which says:

"So do not fear, for I am with you; do not be dismayed, for I am your God. I will strengthen you and help you; I will uphold you with my righteous right hand. For I am the LORD, your God, who takes hold of your right hand and says to you, Do not fear; I will help you."

I have all my journals from that time in my life, documenting all my feelings and prayers. I can see where

8

I wrote one time, "Please give me strength as Mom, Harold, and I approach surgery." I also wrote down Psalm 62:1-2, 5-6 as important verses about calm and peace. That passage reads:

"My soul finds rest in God alone;
my salvation comes from him.
He alone is my rock and my salvation;
he is my fortress, I will never be shaken.
Find rest, O my soul, in God alone;
my hope comes from him.
He alone is my rock and my salvation;
he is my fortress, I will not be shaken."

I read these scriptures repeatedly and prayed over them—even *before* I knew for sure I was the donor. I even emailed several of my friends to pray for the donor to be strong, healthy, and a good match for him. I still have those emails from several friends, and they are so encouraging to read again. We all prayed for the donor long and hard.

Meanwhile, other donors continued to come and go. As time got closer, we were slim on volunteers. Then Ben, my husband at the time, went in for testing. In the meantime, our close family friend, Paul Bass III, offered his kidney as well. Mom has known Paul and his dad all her life. Paul's dad, Paul Bass, Jr., was Mom's best friend throughout her life. They were born six months apart in Tyler, Texas. Paul was an only child, and so was Mom. Their parents were best friends, too. All of Mom's baby pictures were taken with Paul, so they have always thought of themselves as brother and sister. (I even call him Uncle Paul.) One week before the surgery, Paul ended up being a perfect match, and we thought he would be "the" donor. Ben was designated as the "back up" donor. We will always be grateful to both Paul and Ben for their generosity and willingness to donate their kidney to Harold. In this type of surgery, there must always be a back up for the donor, and we would soon find out why.

I went with Ben to see the surgeon before he did his MRI, the last of all the tests. While we waited for the surgeon to arrive, I called Mom to check in. She confirmed that Paul already had a room set up in the hospital and things were going according to plan. Just then, the surgeon came in and began to explain all the details of the surgery. Ben and I sat there listening (or pretending to, since Ben was only the back up). Then the surgeon said, "So, you need to be at the hospital a week from Friday at 5:00am." We perked up our ears.

"Oh wait, Ben's just the back up. We have a donor, Paul Bass."

"He was cut," the surgeon said as he flipped through his chart. "Mr. Bass is no longer the donor; Ben is."

"When was he cut?" I asked, my voice trembling. I'd just talked to my mom and everything was set up for Paul.

"An hour ago. After Mr. Bass's MRI, the doctors decided he was no longer a candidate. Mr. Alford, you are the donor now."

My face went blank as the color drained from my cheeks. Time stopped. I automatically reached down into my purse and grabbed a pen and paper without taking my eyes off the surgeon. Now I was taking notes fast and furiously.

My mind was thinking, "He doesn't know; he must be wrong." Nevertheless, I began asking 50 questions and writing down all the answers. After my barrage of questions, we left the surgeon's office feeling numb. The minute the door closed behind us, I cried out, "He must be wrong, how can this happen?"

Ben was walking ahead of me in silence. He was now the donor, and we were out of volunteers. I fished my cell phone out of my purse and dialed Mom.

"Mom, Paul was cut! Ben is now the donor!" I cried into the phone.

My face went blank as the color drained from my cheeks.

"What are you talking about?" she replied and I explained what the surgeon had said. "Let me call you back," she said. She was calling another doctor to confirm this news.

By now, I was in full panic mode. My emotions were all over the place. Ben and I had only been married three years, and Harold had been my stepdad for over half my life. I didn't feel right about Ben doing this surgery for our family. We were now at the MRI station and Ben was checking in for his test. I was freaking out. He was so calm. As we were sitting in the waiting room, I realized my Bible class was starting in 20 minutes at our house. It was too late to cancel as most of the girls were on their way or already there.

Ben insisted I go home and teach the Bible class. I felt horrible leaving him there all alone to do his MRI, but I went on to the house. As I pulled up, there were two cars in front. Nobody knew about all the chaos that was going on in my life, and I managed to get through my lesson. The minute the girls left, I called Mom for an update.

"So what's the story?" I anxiously hoped that there'd been some mistake and Mom had cleared it up.

"Well, Honey, the surgeon was right...Paul was cut."

I stood there frozen.

She continued, "...and Ben is now the donor. Now, we have to find a back up for Ben. Who should we call?"

Once more, I felt that sense of peace and calmly said, "Mom, it's my turn." She immediately burst into tears.

"I can't let you go! I can't have you and Harold in the hospital at the same time."

"Mom, we've been praying for the perfect donor for two months now. We don't want to mess with God's will, do we?"

"But He doesn't know how I feel!" she said.

"Yes, He does, Mom. I'm totally fine about it, really. I have a sense of peace about it, and I'll be okay. Let me finish my testing, and we can go from there."

We hung up the phone, and in the middle of calamity, another wave of peace washed over me again. I knew I was in God's hands, and I would be okay. He confirmed it through the peace He gave me.

∽

I called the next morning and began a four-day series of tests. One of the tests is an interview with a social worker. Just before she asked me the first question, my cell phone rang. Lately, it seemed as if every time the phone rang it was some kind of bad news.

"Do you need to get that?" she asked politely.

"Yes, it's my mom. I'll be right back," and I dashed out of her office into the hallway.

I talked with Mom briefly and returned to her office. She sat ram rod straight in her chair, her ankles neatly crossed. Her hair was short and perfectly styled like June Cleaver. She had glasses on and was holding a folder with a pen in one hand, ready to capture any sort of stress or anxiety I might indicate regarding the surgery. We sat so close in her tiny office that our knees nearly touched.

"Is everything alright?" she asked, her voice professional and calm.

"Well, our family is in the middle of a tornado right now," I said, referring to the donor situation.

"Oh, the one in Tennessee?" apparently referring to the week's recent weather troubles in the South.

Is she kidding? I thought to myself. "Um, no...I meant what's going on in our family right now."

"Well, let's get started," she decided. "Now Mr. Simmons is your stepdad, is that correct?"

"Yes." She made a note.

"And he is seventy-six years old?"

"Yes." Another note.

Now, she leaned forward and asked in a soft voice, "How would it make you feel if your stepdad did not survive the surgery after you have donated your kidney to him? Do you think that would have an impact on you?"

Without any hesitation I said, "Ma'am, I can tell you this. I wouldn't think twice, even if he only lived for two weeks I would give him my leg, arm, or whatever he needed."

"Uh, okay," she said and skipped over a few pages on her clipboard. "Let's move on to the next session." The rest of the interview was quick and easy.

I knew I was the donor because the Lord had put it on my heart and gave me the peace that surpasses all understanding (Philippians 4:7). And nothing could change my mind.

Even when the doctors told me there was a chance I might not make it and asked if I was sure I wanted to do it, I was certain. All I knew was that I was in the Lord's will, and that's right where I wanted to be. Whether I lived or died, I knew it was His will. I fully trusted Him with my life. If I didn't make it, I knew I was going to heaven, and that was fine with me, too! Therefore, I never had any doubt about doing it. God was in control, and that was a relief.

The following Wednesday, Mom told me the doctor would be calling later that afternoon with all of my test results. I wanted to be there with her and Harold when he called because I knew in my heart I would be the donor. I came in the back door of their house and walked up the stairs. Elna, their house manager, met me in the hallway.

"Where is Mom?" I asked.

"She's in her room, crying."

Right away, I realized the one remaining other potential donor (a lady who had been tested the same week as me) must have been cut. I've only seen Mom cry two or three times in my life—she is such a strong and stable woman. Me? I cry at the drop of a hat. I get that from my dad, Larry; he was like that, too. Slowly, I walked into Mom and Harold's bedroom. Harold was in the middle of his dialysis treatment, lying very still in a hospital bed they had set up at their home. His nurse was beside him, and he was connected to a large machine. Mom was rubbing his feet.

"Hi, Honey," Mom said, mustering up a smile for me. Harold and the nurse joined in a cheery greeting as well.

"How are you feeling, Harold?" I asked, standing beside him.

Whether I lived or died, I knew it was His will.

"Oh, pretty good," he responded, his voice tired.

"Well," Mom began, "the other donor was cut today, so we are waiting for the doctor to call with your results." Ben was already the back up donor—we knew that. Now I was about to find out where I fit into the equation. But I felt I already knew the answer.

About that time, the phone rang. Mom and I went into another room so she could pick it up at her desk. I sat on the other side of her desk listening.

"Hello? Yes, he's doing okay today…" I knew it was the doctor calling about Harold. "So, who is the best donor?"

I looked at Mom as she heard the doctor's response,

and her eyes filled with tears. I knew he had said my name. She leaned her head back on her chair, put her hand on her forehead and said, "How in the world could it come down to the two people I prayed it wouldn't be?" I'm not sure what the doctor's response was to that question; it was probably the first time he had been asked that. She hung up the phone and said, "It's you," her hands on her cheeks.

"Mom, I'm totally fine," I assured her, telling her once more about this strong sense of peace I'd had the entire time. "I'll be alright," I added as I felt another tinge of peace come my way.

"Well, let's go tell Harold," Mom said and stood to her feet. We walked back into the room where Harold was and Mom said, "Well, Ben and Amy are both good matches."

Harold turned to me and said with his characteristic humor, "You gonna flip a coin to see who gets to give their kidney?" Mom smiled softly and went back to rubbing his feet, hesitating only a moment before she spoke.

"Honey, Amy has decided she wants to do it."

Harold extended his arms, and I walked over to hug him, being careful with the tubes and plugs. We hugged, and he had tears streaming down his face; we all did. He said, "I love you so much, thank you."

"I'm happy to do it," I answered. "I love you, too." I truly was happy to be the one. Harold had been so sweet, kind, and generous to me all my life. I could never repay him for all the things he'd given me—trips, college, and so much more. But more than the material things, his love and kindness towards me as his stepdaughter had been the best gift. He went through all my rebellious, selfish, wild, and crazy years…and still loved me. The least I could do was to give him life!

As I sat there looking at him, I realized he'd already saved so many lives through his loving heart and generous donations to people, hospitals, and research. In that moment, I was certain that he could do more for the people in our country in two years than I could do the rest of my lifetime! "Well, I need to go home and talk to Ben," I said, turning to leave.

"Okay, Honey. Call if you need us," Mom said, recalling a phrase I've heard all my life. But now it held special meaning as I realized how blessed I am to have parents who love me, care about me, and want to help me—even when they need help.

In less than two minutes, I was back home. Ben was waiting for me. I said I needed to update him on what was going on, so Ben poured us a glass of wine. I put together some cheese and crackers, and we sat in our den by the fire. I took a deep breath and began to explain what had transpired over the last two hours. We sat on the sofa for at least another two or three hours, discussing what was going to happen in the next few days.

I had never had surgery before, but I was so eager to do this for Harold, no matter the outcome. I was able to convince Ben to let me be the donor, and he remained the back up. After all, I reasoned, he is *my* stepdad. Who knows? Ben might need to give his kidney to one of his family members someday.

By the time we finished talking and praying about it, it was close to 8:00 in the evening on Wednesday, February 20. The surgery was scheduled for 5:00am that Friday. I had one day to cancel photo shoots, meetings, and organize the house to receive guests who might stop by after the surgery.

Next, I sent out an email to the 40 prayer warriors that had been praying for "the perfect donor." I wrote, "I want to thank you all for praying for the perfect donor for Harold. As of today, it's going to be me! So thank you for praying *for me!*" Immediately, I began receiving calls and encouraging emails. My sweet friend, Paige, organized two weeks of meals during my recovery. So many friends joined in and brought some of my favorite dishes like banana pudding, chicken spaghetti, and macaroni and cheese, to name a few!

The night before the surgery, Mom arranged for us to have dinner at the country club with my brother and his family. (They too had offered kidneys but were not a perfect match). It was a joyful time with the family, and we made several toasts to a successful surgery and quick recovery. As we began to leave, we all hugged each other tight and said "I love you" a thousand times. I remember that moment as if it were yesterday.

Four o'clock the next morning came quickly, but I was rested, prayed up, and ready to go! When we arrived at Baylor Hospital, someone was there to greet us and take us to a prep room where I exchanged my clothes for a backless robe. I was sitting on the bed waiting when David, Ben's youngest brother, walked through the door. He just happened to be in Dallas on business that day and found us! He lives a few hours away in Henderson, Texas, with his wife, Fran, and their two daughters. I was glad to see him, and he helped keep my mind off what was about to happen. I have a difficult time with needles and IVs. Before I knew it, there were about nine friends in this tiny space. John Maisel, the president of East West Ministries and a good friend of ours, asked to pray for me. We joined hands in a circle around my bed with Ben, David, Andy, Penny, Paige, Courtney, and "Little A" (my niece, Adrienne). John began to pray an inspiring and encouraging prayer. My emotions took over, and I felt tears filling my eyes. He prayed for the Lord's protection from infection and asked that we would be completely healed. He also prayed for God to guide the doctors and nurses in surgery.

To break up the seriousness of the moment afterwards, the nurse came in and gave me a "party hat" that looked like a shower cap! I donned my hat

> **We all hugged each other tight and said "I love you" a thousand times.**

and transferred to a different hospital bed with wheels. I was thankful my young niece was there, or I would have burst into tears right then. But I was holding it together because I didn't want to scare her by seeing Aunt Aim crying or emotional. I wanted to be strong for her. Paige put a coat of my favorite pink lip gloss on as they wheeled me down the hall. Everyone was waving goodbye and saying, "We love you…see you in a couple hours!"

I couldn't tell it, but my friends were crying. Ben walked alongside me holding my hand. "How do I look?" I asked with a smile. It's hard to look cute in a shower cap, but thank goodness I had my pink lip gloss!

"You look great," he said and squeezed my hand. Inside the "pre-op" room, Mom, Harold, my brother, and Uncle Paul were there with the doctors and me. Gary Brandenburg, our pastor, was there to pray over me before they took me back. My family surrounded my hospital bed. Gary was holding my left hand; Mom was holding my right. As Gary began to pray, Mom gasped. I opened my eyes and saw her put her other hand over her mouth. All of this was just about more than she could take. Everyone had tears in their eyes, including me.

After that, the cute anesthesiologist sat beside me and explained what was going to happen next. I jokingly called what he was going to give me the "goo-goo" juice, and within seconds after the injection I was happy and calm. They could have been wheeling me to a furnace, and I would have smiled the whole way. I said goodbye to everyone as they took me down the hall to the operating room.

Once I was in surgery, Harold began his pre-op routine. All along, I'd pictured us going into the operating room together, lying side-by-side and holding hands with our shower caps on like Thelma and Louise. But it wasn't like that at all. I went first, and they removed my left kidney. By then, Harold was prepped and ready, and they literally walked my kidney down the hall to his operating room and put it inside of Harold. Sounds easy, but there was a lot more to it than that! The cuts had to be 100% precise in this very intricate surgery. The surgeons went through the front of my abdomen near the bikini line and through the torso to the back where the kidney is located and pulled it back through the front side.

About 200 of Mom and Harold's friends were anxiously waiting for each doctor's report on me, but mostly about him. Some flew from Santa Barbara to be there for Mom and Harold. Needless to say, they are loved and have many friends who care deeply for them. Mom had secured a hospital room next to Harold's with a sliding partition so she could check on him. While she sat there in the quiet, waiting for the doctor to tell her Harold was out of surgery, a big man with a bright smile came in to clean the room. He saw Mom sitting on the side of the bed, her hands clasped together between her knees.

"Ma'am, how ya doing?" he asked as he emptied the trashcan and went about his duties.

Mom looked up at the unsuspecting man and let out an uncontrollable, ugly cry, "My husband and daughter are both in surgery! My daughter is giving her kidney to my husband!"

"I'm sorry," he offered sheepishly. "I didn't mean to do that to you." He didn't know what to do for a moment, then he said, "My gosh…I need to go get my phone and call my church to pray for them!" And off he went! He came back in a few minutes and said, "Ma'am, the whole church is prayin' for you." They were instant friends. Claude was his name. He came and checked on Mom and Harold every day they were in the hospital. He even came to visit me, but I don't remember meeting him because I slept so much after surgery!

In the recovery room, I remember opening my eyes

and seeing Ben standing over me. "Is Harold okay?" I wanted to know.

"Yes, he is doing well," Ben assured me.

Madeline, Ben's youngest daughter, was standing beside him. I felt as if I were in a dream, but at the same time, I knew where I was and what had just happened.

Before I arrived in my hospital room, my longtime friend, Margot, had de-germed the room with Clorox wipes (that's what friends are for)! The next thing I remember was being in my newly sanitized room with the nurses, dozing in and out of sleep. Before the surgery, I had written out some verses that gave me hope and security. Ben put them on my bulletin board in my hospital room. I was clinging to these verses up until the surgery, including the one my friend had emailed me so long ago from Psalm 57:1 that said:

"Have mercy on me, O God, have mercy on me, for in you my soul takes refuge. I will take refuge in the shadow of your wings until the disaster has passed."

Mom made sure the nurses who took care of me received a signed copy of my book in hopes that it might encourage them. They were all so nice and helpful to me during my recovery. The entire staff at Baylor Hospital was friendly and anxious to help wherever they could.

The next morning, I woke up and Ben was there on the sofa waiting for me to open my eyes. "How are you feeling?"

"Okay. How's Harold?" I couldn't get my stepdad out of my mind.

"He's doing great…he's in his room."

About that time, my brother came in to see me. "Hey, how are you?" he asked and stood at the end of my bed.

"Good…moving slow. Have you seen Harold today?" I had visions of Harold being as out of it as I was.

"He was up walking around the 14ᵗʰ floor earlier," my brother said.

That's nice, I thought. "What? He's walking?" I couldn't get out of bed, much less walk.

"He's lapped the 14ᵗʰ floor a couple of times," my brother said, grinning.

"Call the doctor!" I cried. "Something is wrong with me! I can't even get out of bed!" Our physician came in soon after my panicked request. He explained, "Amy, you're perfectly fine! It's much harder on the donor than it is on the recipient. We will get you up to walk in a couple of hours."

> I had written out some verses that gave me hope and security.

A team of people came in after lunch and sat me in a wheelchair so I could go from the 12ᵗʰ floor to the 14ᵗʰ to see Harold for the first time. They wheeled me into the room, and I saw he was in a hospital robe that matched mine. We were both in wheelchairs, so Ben and Mom helped us stand up to hug each other and say, "I love you."

Harold asked me if I wanted to go for a walk. We walked down the hallway, hand-in-hand, Andy pushing the cart behind us with all of Harold's tubes and medicines. Mom was holding me, and Ben was close behind taking photos. It was a sweet and tender moment and one I will always treasure—especially the photographs Ben took of us. He even got a great shot the next day of Harold and I walking and holding hands. Mom was right behind us, faithfully toting a big cup of banana pudding and a spoon. Harold was so thin—she was trying to get him to gain back some weight. So she followed him just in case he would have a hankering for some pudding!

For the four days I was in the hospital, my sweet mom walked up and down the stairs back and forth to visit my room two floors below Harold's. The elevators took too long for Mom, so she took the stairs. Thank goodness she is a spry seventy-three-year-old! When it was time to go home, Mom, a nurse, and a doctor helped me out to the car. When we arrived home, Ben helped me get into my own bed. It was great to be home, but I hated not being close to Harold and Mom. He would be in the hospital for two more days. I now had a special bond with Harold and Mom and didn't want to be away from them.

While Ben was working upstairs in our house, my friends took turns babysitting me. I needed help in and out of bed, walking, and sitting. Everyone was so sweet and gracious to help. I must have had 30 or 40 flower arrangements and more food than I could ever eat. My best friend, Cara, flew in from Arkansas to spend two nights with me. We loved our quiet time together, not blowing and going like we usually do on a visit. Instead, we sat on the sofa or on the bed and talked and watched a movie or two. The doctors said I needed to begin walking every day, so she helped me walk down the street. The first time we walked, we were arm-in-arm taking slow, short steps. I joked, "This will be us in 40 years." We laughed, which kind of hurt my side, so I tried not to laugh anymore. But it is hard not to laugh when you are with your best friends.

The day Cara left, I cried and cried. I wanted her to stay, but she needed to get home to her own kids and husband. I was very grateful, and it meant so much that she came to take care of me. Mom and Harold stopped by to see me on their way home from the hospital. Harold looked 1000 times better. His color had improved, and he didn't seem so weak. It warmed my heart.

A week after the surgery, Mom and Harold had us over to their house for dinner. It was my first outing since I came home, and I decided to dress in a red leather jacket. I never wear red. That jacket is the only red item I have in my closet. Ben helped me through the back door when we got to Mom's, and Harold was standing there in the hall. I couldn't believe my eyes! He was wearing a bright red vest (a color he rarely wears either)! I said, "Oh my gosh, it's the kidney!" We were now thinking alike! What's really funny is we have to go to the bathroom at the same time now!

We celebrated our one-month anniversary, then our one-year anniversary. As of February 22, 2010, it's been two years since our surgery. Both Harold and I are doing great. He was back in the office just a week after the surgery and continues to play golf several times a week. (Thank you, Lord!)

∞

As I look back at the kidney transplant, I realize God knew when Mom married Harold 30 years ago I would be his donor. Over the last 20 years, my relationship with the Lord has grown and strengthened above and beyond what I ever thought it would be. Sandy, my mentor, has had a big part in teaching me over the years to trust God, depend on Him for everything, and be available to Him for His purposes. Had I not learned that from Sandy's teachings, I am not sure I would have been so eager and glad to be Harold's donor. Because I asked God for His will, not mine, He provided a peace, comfort, and assurance that gave me the confidence and encouragement to go through this knowing I was in His hands. He was in control, and that made it easy for me to be the donor. I knew in my heart I was where God wanted me to be—in His will. Throughout the entire ordeal, I was never scared, worried, or afraid, and I never thought twice about doing it. I will never regret it.

I would not trade the past two years spending time with Harold and Mom for anything. God blessed me for obeying Him and desiring to be in His will. My relationship with the Lord has increased tenfold since the kidney transplant. Make that a hundred fold. I know for a fact that nothing is impossible with God. The Bible teaches us that, but I was fortunate enough to learn it from my own experience. Now I know He is real, and He does give us peace in the middle of our trials.

Ephesians 2:8-10 says, "For it is by grace you have been saved, through faith—and this not from yourselves, it is the gift of God—not by works, so that no one can boast. For we are God's workmanship, created in Christ

Jesus to do good works, which God prepared in advance for us to do." This verse clearly says we are saved because of our faith in Christ. It's because we accept Him and believe He alone is our Savior—not Buddha, not a statue—but Jesus Christ Himself. You cannot get to heaven because you are a good person. You cannot get to heaven because you donate to charities and give to the poor. It is by your faith, not what you "do." It is not even by donating a kidney—but by your faith.

The Bible says we were created in Christ Jesus to do "good works." Sure, the good works are great, don't get me wrong, but it's your belief in Jesus Christ that really matters. The last part of that passage in Ephesians says, "...which God prepared in advance for us to do." He knew I was going to donate my kidney before I was born! It was His plan all along, and because I was available to Him to be in His will, He covered me in peace.

He was in control, and that made it easy for me to be the donor.

Philippians 4:6–7 reminds us, "Do not be anxious about anything (even giving up your kidney), but in everything (not just the big things, everything), by prayer and petition, with thanksgiving, present your requests to God. (Ask Him to help you in your time of need, tell Him how you feel and what encouragement or peace you want from Him.) And the peace of God, which transcends all understanding, will guard your hearts and minds in Christ Jesus" (parentheses added). That verse perfectly explains what happened to me! I prayed, made my requests known to God, and His peace guarded my mind.

I cannot explain the amount of peace I felt the morning of my surgery; it was above comprehension. As I've said, He protected me from being anxious, nervous, or afraid. First Peter 5:7 says, "Cast all (not just a few things, but *all*) your anxiety on him (Why?) because he cares for you" (parentheses added). This is another verse telling us to give Him all our stress, troubles, and anxiety because He cares for those who love and believe in Him. Just a few chapters earlier in 1 Peter 1:2, the Bible says, "Grace and peace be yours in abundance through the knowledge of God and of Jesus our Lord." If you don't read the Bible or Scripture, how can you know what the Lord has for you? The more you know about Christ, the more you will begin to trust Him, and He will give you His grace and peace in abundance. My friend, Joy, always says, "How can you know what you don't know?" It's true! You don't have to take my word for it in this story; read the Bible because it is true, and learn all that the Lord has for you as a believer in Jesus Christ.

DANCING AT THE SWEETHEART BALL

THE ANNUAL FUNDRAISER FOR THE CARDIOLOGY Department at UT Southwestern in Dallas is called the Sweetheart Ball. It's by far the most beautiful and elaborate party of the year with a great dinner (and a live band afterwards to dance off the calories!). I don't normally attend this party, but one year a longtime friend was chairing the event and asked me several times to go. When she told me the guests who would be sitting at our table, I decided to go because I'd be with a great group of people. Sure enough, the party was over-the-top incredible—far beyond any party I'd ever attended!

After dinner, Harold came over from across the room and asked me to dance. (He always asks me to dance to the "fast" songs because Mom prefers the slow ones!) This was only a few months after our surgery, but we began to boogie! It didn't bother either one of us that we were the only ones on the dance floor (at least, I don't recall anyone else being there!). We were really cuttin' a rug, as we say in Texas, and having fun. Harold loves dancing. He throws his arms high above his head and occasionally lets out a "woo-hoo." He moves more than most of my friends' husbands, and he is seventy-seven years old! About halfway through the song, I noticed almost everyone was watching us dance. They were smiling, some with tears in their eyes. Couples whispered to one another and exchanged knowing looks. I remember thinking that they either thought we were horrible dancers and looked like fools, or they were talking about what we'd just gone through together.

We danced our way through two or three songs and had a great time. When the music slowed down, we returned to our seats and continued on with the night.

The next day, several people called my mom to tell her what an incredible moment it was to see Harold and me dancing together just two months after our kidney transplant! "There was not a dry eye at our table," one lady said. "Everyone was so touched when they saw them dancing. She gave him his life back." So, they weren't making fun of our dancing after all! They were amazed at his recovery. It made the memories of that fabulous night even more special, if that were possible. It will always be a special moment in my life to think back on how sick Harold was just two months prior, and look at him now!

This story reminds me that God is faithful to his children. Are you a child of God? You are if you have put your trust and faith in Him. If you have done that, you can know God is with you and will fulfill all His promises. If you're not sure you can trust God right now, ask God to reveal His faithfulness to you. Someday, I hope you will do as I did that night at the party and reflect on all God has done and be certain of His absolute faithfulness. Why not start today by thanking the Lord for all He has done for you? Take some time to write down five blessings He has given you, and thank Him for each one.

"For nothing is impossible with God." Luke 1:37

When God Intervenes in PRAYER

GOD IS NEVER LATE...
AND SELDOM EARLY

ASPEN, COLORADO, IS ONE OF MY FAVORITE PLACES IN the world. When I go to Aspen in the summers, I get re-charged in my faith, and my walk with the Lord strengthens. I'll sit on my balcony or porch for hours, praying, reading the Bible, or just looking up at the mountains praising God for the opportunity to be able to come to such a beautiful place. A lot of times when I'm talking to God and thanking Him for everything, the tears start flowing. I feel an overwhelming sense of peace and joy in my soul that causes my eyes to well up in tears. There is something about being in the mountains; maybe it's because I'm closer to God...about 8000 feet closer! I've experienced His provision in so many big and small ways in Aspen, including an episode with a friend who needed to sell her truck.

About six years ago, my good friend, Melissa, was trying to sell her 1989 two-wheel drive Blazer (along with her condo) in Aspen. We both lived in Dallas, and I was planning to go up to Aspen for a month that summer. "Hey Mel," I asked her one day, "I have a proposition for you. If you will let me use your truck in Aspen for the month of July, I'll try to sell it for you while I'm there. That way you won't have to worry about it."

"Sounds great!" she agreed. "But what if you sell it

right away? Then you won't have anything to drive." I was staying in Aspen through the end of July and needed transportation.

"I'll figure something out," I said. "Or I'll just tell the buyer they can't have it until July 31." She wasn't sure that idea would go over so well, since most people would also want to have it for the summer.

"I bet I can work it out," I assured her. That summer, I had been spending a lot of time in prayer. I was growing closer to God and learning to trust Him with everything.

"Alright, girlfriend. Go for it," she said.

I put "For Sale" signs on the truck and placed an ad in the *Aspen Times*. Every day I prayed, "Lord, please bring the perfect person to buy this truck. But You know I need some wheels, so please bring them towards the end of the month." I knew God had a plan, and I was hoping it would accommodate my timing. Three weeks went by, and I only had one looker. Nobody wants a two-wheel drive in Colorado—they're all looking for four-wheel drive to go off-road or use in the snow. When I was halfway through July, Melissa and I started discussing Plan B.

"If we don't sell it, I'll hire someone from Denver to drive it to Dallas," she offered, thinking we'd have a much better chance of selling the truck in Dallas. I couldn't imagine how much that would cost her, and I started feeling guilty that I had used the car all month without anyone making an offer. As the fourth and final week rolled around, I arranged for my "Aspen" friend, Julie, to keep the truck until we could find someone to drive it to Dallas. On July 31, my last day in Aspen, Julie and I drove in the truck to the Aspen airport to drop me off. My mom and Harold (who is a pilot) were flying in to pick me up on their way home. Julie and I sat on the tarmac in the truck, watching my parents' plane approaching.

"Knock, knock, knock," suddenly another pilot was standing outside the truck window, knocking on the glass. I rolled down the window as Mom and Harold taxied down the runway.

"Hi, is your truck for sale?" he asked.

Julie burst out laughing, and we both said, "Yes!"

"My son needs a truck, and he lives in California," the pilot explained, taking a look around the truck. "This would be perfect for him." God brought me the perfect buyer, with only three minutes to spare. We traded phone numbers as I hugged Julie goodbye. She just shook her head and said, "What timing! You sure have a good connection with the guy upstairs!"

This is just one of the many times the Lord intervened and answered my prayers. It was in His timing, and it was by far the best timing! I don't take His answers to my prayers for granted. Every situation like that builds my faith more and more and strengthens my "connection" with God, as my friend said. I have that connection because I have a *relationship* with Him. Christianity is not a set of rules to follow—that's religion. Christianity is a real love relationship with Him. Sandy once told me, "Do not put your trust in religion, but put your trust in Christ." If you put your faith in Jesus, you too will enjoy a good connection with Him and see Him answer your prayers like He has answered mine.

Ring, Ring!
It's God Calling!

I HAD BEEN IN TYLER'S ICU WITH BEN'S PARENTS, Phyllis and Landon, for three days. His mother had undergone emergency brain surgery as the result of falling the week prior. To make matters worse, Fran, Ben's sister-in-law, had just been diagnosed with stage 3 breast cancer as well. We live two hours away in Dallas, but my friend Jackie is from Tyler and graciously allowed us to stay in her guest home while we helped Ben's family. However, soon after we settled in at her place, Jackie called in despair saying, "My dad was just diagnosed with stage 3 stomach cancer." Her mom had died of cancer 10 years ago, and she was devastated by this sudden news. I myself was feeling overwhelmed with all the crises seeming to pop up all around me.

I started helping Jackie by making phone calls to M.D. Anderson and UT Southwestern to try to get her dad in as soon as possible. He had already hit the road that day to drive from Arkansas to Texas to live with Jackie while he underwent treatment. In the middle of my flurry of phone calls, she called with even worse news. Her dad had flipped his pick-up truck five times on the highway and landed upside down in a creek beside the road! All his clothes and belongings had been strewn all over the ground and the creek. His son, who was driving behind him, witnessed the whole thing. Somehow, Mike wrestled his dad out of the twisted, mangled wreckage, but the helicopter care flight could not land because of fog. Father and son waited for an ambulance instead and finally made it to the same Tyler hospital where I had been all week.

That's when I fell apart. This was the fourth major tragedy that had happened in about eight days. Amid all of this, another friend's child had shot herself and was in ICU, struggling to live (and find the desire to live). Not only that, this same friend's sister-in-law had been rushed to the hospital for immediate surgery to remove a brain tumor they'd just discovered.

I began crying and prayed out loud for all these people who were suffering. Then I did what I often do whenever I am stressed out—I called Sandy, who is like an adopted

> This was the fourth major tragedy that had happened in about eight days.

grandmother, friend and mentor to me all rolled into one. She quietly reminded me, "God's in control, and He is faithful." Whenever we talk, I'm usually holding the phone in one hand and a pen in the other so I can write down in my journal the bits of godly wisdom she shares. I took four pages of notes that day. She reminded me that God permitted all of this to happen. And He has a purpose for each disaster—His purpose is that He gets the glory. "We don't know why a problem happens, but He solves it and resolves it," she added. "Leave it in His hands."

Sandy helped me to see the truth. God didn't say we would understand our problems; He only said,

"Trust Me." I knew that God needed to be the One I was looking to for help. Nothing in my "flesh" could bring me the peace that only He can bring. Philippians 4:6-7 says, "Do not be anxious about anything, but in everything, by prayer and petition, with thanksgiving, present your requests to God. And the peace of God, which transcends all understanding, will guard your hearts and your minds in Christ Jesus." Later in that same chapter, Paul adds, "I can do everything through him who gives me strength" (verse 13). This means I can bear everything with His strength.

Jesus asked in Matthew 6:27, "Who of you by worrying can add a single hour to his life?" We don't understand why God permits these things to happen, but we do know He wants us to come to Him in our time of need. Each trial strengthens our faith more, if we trust and obey Him. "You will see the results, and your faith will increase," Sandy assured me.

While we were talking, someone else called me, but I didn't answer because I didn't recognize the phone number. About an hour and a half later, I remembered to listen to the message. It was a new friend I'd met in a Bible study and had only spoken to her once in the last two months. "Hey Amy, this is Susan McCord," her message began. "I just wanted to call you and let you know I'm praying for you. I know you have a lot on your plate right now, and I felt God's push to call you." I was stunned. How did she know? Then she added, "I'm actually in Bible study right now and stepped out into the hall to call you...just know I'm praying for you."

That may have been Susan on the line, but I knew it

was a call from God! He was letting me know that He had not abandoned me or forgotten me. The next morning, I woke up at four and felt Him impress on me again, "That was Me calling you." He reminded me that He is there for us even when it seems as if everything else is falling apart.

BUSTER, THE BEST DOG IN THE WORLD

BUSTER WAS MY BLACK-AND-WHITE ENGLISH SPRINGER spaniel and the love of my life. "Bus," one of the nicknames I called him, was the best dog in the world; not to mention the most regal, handsome, perfect dog. His mom was "Spackel," and they looked like twins, but I could always tell them apart. They loved each other so much—always playing, kissing each other, and cuddling together on their bed. I have several thousand photos of Spackel and Buster. (Okay, I am a photographer *and* a dog lover!)

I've always loved dogs, even at two years old. "Mixy," my first dog, was my everything at that age. I loved Spackel, but Buster was my true love. He rode in my car with me everywhere I went. He had "his spot" in the Ford Explorer I drove. His chest would lean on the middle console between the two seats in front—his left paw on my seat, his right paw on the right seat. This position was perfect. It held him in place when Mommy would go around the corners on two wheels. He placed his face perfectly positioned in front of the AC vents to get the maximum amount of cool air (which also gave him full view out the windshield for any possible squirrel sightings). He was so smart to figure that out!

Buster went through so many difficult things with me: my divorce, my dad's death, my engagement to another man (who didn't like Buster or Spackel), my broken engagement (which thrilled everyone, including Buster and Spackel), a very stressful trial my family endured, and Spackel's death. In the summer of 1998, I was living alone in my first home in Dallas. One early Saturday morning, I went out to the front yard to water my impatiens. I was still in my boxers and t-shirt, and Spackel and Buster tumbled out the door together with me. They never left my yard, preferring to stick close to Mommy. While I was watering the flowers, I heard the soundtrack of my worst nightmare: a thump, tires screeching, and a dog yelping. Everything seemed to happen in slow motion as I spun around and saw Buster lying in the street. His screaming and yelping was the worst sound I've ever heard. I ran to him and stood over his mangled, bloody body. We made eye contact, and it was as if he were saying, "Mommy, help me! Help me!"

I immediately scooped him up in my arms. He stopped crying the minute I picked him up. His body, however, was still contorted. Out of the corner of my eye, I saw the car that ran over him turn around and pull up next to me.

"Amy, get in," the driver urged.

"Who is this person?" I thought. "How does she know me?" But Buster needed to go to the vet immediately, so I opened her back door, still holding Buster. I got into the car, called to Spackel to jump in with us, and I shut the door. A blood-curdling yelp came from Spackel. I had shut the door on her tail. I opened the door, got her tail out of the way, and shut it again.

"Amy, where should I go?" the driver asked, terrified. I then realized she was my neighbor who lived a few houses down.

"There's a vet on Mockingbird and Skillman... Hurry!" I yelled at the top of my lungs.

"I'm so sorry. I never saw him. I'm so, so sorry," she kept repeating, visibly upset.

Tears streaming down my face, my cries were uncontrollable. My heart was breaking, and I began to pray out loud, "Lord, please don't take Buster. Please Lord, I'm begging You. Not now. Please don't let him die." I prayed the entire ride there, and my

> I heard the soundtrack of my worst nightmare: a thump, tires screeching, and a dog yelping.

voice grew louder and louder as we approached the vet. We pulled up to the front door, and I jumped out with Buster's lifeless body in my arms. I kicked the double doors open, covered in blood, and yelled, "I need a doctor!" Everyone turned and stared in disbelief.

The girls behind the counter jumped up quickly to show me where to go. I had never been to this place. I knew my vet very well, but his clinic was too far to drive in Buster's condition. They raced me to the back where they perform surgeries and told me to put Buster on the table. Just as I did, he launched into a full-blown seizure. His front legs went totally stiff, his back rounded upwards. The vet techs were telling me to leave, saying they would take care of him. Distraught and still crying, I refused to leave.

One girl grabbed me by the arm and said, "You have to leave now. We can't start working on him while you're back here." Meanwhile, Buster was having a seizure, I thought he was dying, and I was trying to hold him on the table. I answered her, "Buster has always been there for me. I'm *not* leaving him when he needs me the most! Do what you have to do. I'll stand right here, but I'm not leaving him." At that point, they gave up trying to make me leave.

As promised, I stood back as they held him down and treated the huge spots of open flesh. They used staples to stop the bleeding all over his chest and legs where he had road rash. I could see the black tire marks that started on his stomach between his legs and traveled all the way up his white fur to his neck. I guess his head was to the side, and the tire missed it completely. His hind leg was injured. He held it up in the air and wouldn't walk on it. After they treated his wounds the best they could, they put him in a cage about four feet off the ground—just high enough for me to lean inside and wrap my arms around his body.

I put my head next to his and whispered, "Lord, please, don't take Bus Bus. You know how much I love him. Please, Lord, don't take him now." My tears were rolling past my cheeks, along my throat, and down into chest. I was still covered in blood, but I couldn't have cared less. Buster was all I cared about at that moment. The vet came over to me after about 20 minutes, put her hand on my shoulder and told me, "Let's wait until the end of the day to do X-rays."

I knew what she meant. "Let's see if he lives through the day before we do x-rays." She also mentioned there was probably internal bleeding, based on the tire mark stretching from one end of his body to the other. I still refused to leave Buster's side. I called Mom, who loves animals as much as I do, to tell her about the nightmare I was living and asked her to pray. Then I called my brother to tell him what had happened. We'd made plans that day, and I needed to cancel. He brought me a sandwich to eat—I had been at the vet since nine that morning.

All day long, I leaned in the cage and sang praise and worship songs over Buster. I prayed when I wasn't singing. I loved on him like I'd never see him again, and, quite frankly, I wasn't so sure I would. Now I knew how my parents felt when I was in pain. All day, he whimpered and cried. It broke my heart, but I continued singing songs like "Jesus Loves Me" so he would know I was there.

At 4:00, the vet agreed to do the X-rays. I was thrilled, but scared. *What if his leg, hip, or back was broken? Then what, a doggy cast?* They had to stretch his little weak body out on the cold, hard X-ray table. They allowed me to help them. We waited patiently for the results. Now my prayer was, "Lord, please, no internal bleeding, no broken bones. Let him live." Over and over, I prayed for that. Soon, the vet came in and said with a puzzled look, "Well, no signs of broken bones or dislocated hips. Everything looks good."

I couldn't believe my ears! "Everything looks good?" I asked. I wanted to hear her say it again. "Thank you Lord!" I cried out. "Thank you so much!

"Of course, we better keep him overnight for observation," she added.

I knew that wasn't going to happen. "I'll observe him at home," I said. "What do I need to do?" She had heard I was pretty persistent, I suppose, so she didn't try arguing with me.

"Well, make sure you wake him each hour. He needs pills every four hours, and take him out to the bathroom. Check to see if there is blood in his urine, and come back tomorrow morning."

We made it through the night. Both Spackel and I were great nurses. She was so glad to see him and cleaned his face over and over with lots of "love licks." She knew something had happened and was very gentle and attentive.

The next morning, we went to the vet's office. She came in the exam room and listened to his heart. Whenever one of us pressed on his chest, we could feel and hear all the bones cracking. It was bizarre. However, he checked out fine. She couldn't believe it. I said to her, "Do you believe in God?"

There was a long silence, so I spoke up. "If you don't, this should change your mind. This is a miracle that he lived and has no broken bones, don't you think?"

"Yes. I believe so," was all she could say. There was no other explanation. God heard my cry for help and intervened. He must have. Was Buster just a "lucky dog"? Well, in some ways, yes. I treated him like a king, but as far as surviving a tire rolling over the length of a dog's body, you have to credit God with that one. Still to this day, I give God the glory for saving Buster on that summer Saturday morning.

Buster totally recovered from the incident and lived another six years. I never took one day for granted that he was alive. I know God gave him another lease on life, and that was His answer to my prayer. Buster is buried at my farm, up on a hill overlooking our lake, facing the sunset. Next to his grave is Spackel, Gracie, and Titus (Mom's dogs), and Beau, my niece Adrienne's cocker spaniel. They all have little headstones with their names and the dates they were born and passed away.

Buster has a large rectangle grave bordered in river rock with beautiful flowers inside. A three-foot iron cross is at the top of his grave, and the headstone reads:

Buster
Buster, you brought us so much joy.
You were there for me during the toughest times
and the happiest times of my life. We will always
remember you. Thank You, Lord, for blessing us with
13 wonderful years with Bus Bus.

Almost every time I go to the farm, my new dog "Buddy" and I visit Buster's grave. Buddy runs around, and I enjoy the beauty of the place. Sometimes I sit beside Buster's grave with my morning coffee and say my prayers. As Buddy gets older, he looks more and more like Buster.

I had adopted the little black-and-white Springer when he was four months old as a companion for Buster in his old age. I hoped his youth would help Buster live longer, and I think it did. I even sent out "announcement" cards (as a joke) to let everyone know I had a new child in my home. It took three weeks for

Buster to accept Buddy as his housemate. (Buddy started out being a little brat.) Eventually, they became the best of friends. Buddy loved Buster and took great care of him, especially during the last year of his life when Buster was half-deaf and half-blind. Whenever I called the dogs to come in from the yard, Buddy would go to Buster, bump him and lead him back to me. It was so cute to see Buddy's love for Buster and how he acquired all of Buster's great traits. Buddy has certainly stepped into Buster's paws, but Buster will never be forgotten.

Buddy has now earned the title, "Best Dog in the World," and I thank the Lord each day for him. He, along with all my other dogs, has brought such joy in my life. To me, dogs are just one more bonus God gives to bring us joy while we are here on earth. The entire time I have been writing this story (and this book for the most part) Buddy has been curled up beside me, resting his head on my lap. He is my 60-pound lap dog, and I'm so blessed to have him with me everywhere I go!

Jesus taught us to be persistent in pursuing God—as persistent as I was in the vet's office that day. Sometimes, we give up after a half-hearted effort. Or, if we don't see an answer right away, we quit praying. To know God takes faith. You must believe He exists. Don't give up when you are seeking God. Ask Him for wisdom and knowledge, patience and understanding, and He will give it to you.

Matthew 7:7 reminds us, "Ask, and it will be given to you; seek, and you will find; knock, and the door will be opened to you. For everyone who asks, receives; he who seeks, finds; and to him who knocks, the door will be opened." God tells us to "ask," and when the car hit

Buster, I asked for his life from the bottom of my heart, with everything I had. I knew God could heal Buster if He wanted to do so. God can do anything He wants: heal the sick, calm the winds, and even bring us peace in the middle of our most difficult situations.

L et the following scriptures encourage you to keep praying and asking God for an answer:

Matthew 8:1-3 "When Jesus came down from the mountainside, large crowds followed him. A man with leprosy came and knelt before him and said, 'Lord, if you are willing, you can make me clean.' (Notice the man didn't say, "Heal me right now, I want to be healed!") Jesus reached out His hand and touched the man. 'I am willing,' he said. 'Be clean!' Immediately he was cured of his leprosy." Sometimes God answers our prayers immediately. Sometimes we have to wait, but His timing is always perfect…even if we don't think so.

Jesus taught us to be persistent in pursuing God.

Psalm 91:14-15 "Because he loves me," says the Lord, "I will rescue him; I will protect him, for he acknowledges my name. He will call upon me, and I will answer him: I will be with him in trouble, I will deliver him and honor him." Try substituting your own name in place of "him" and "he" in this verse to make it more personal. For example: "Because **Amy** loves me," says the Lord, "I will rescue **her**; I will protect **Amy**, for **she** acknowledges my name…"

Psalm 100:1-2 "Shout for joy to the Lord, all the earth. Worship the Lord with gladness; come before him with joyful songs…" (Reminds me of singing over Buster.)

Psalm 100:4-5 "…give thanks to him and praise his name. For the Lord is good and his love endures forever; his faithfulness continues through all generations."

Psalm 102:1-2. "Hear my prayer, O Lord; let my cry for help come to you. Do not hide your face from me when I am in distress. Turn your ear to me; when I call, answer me quickly."

Psalm 105:4-5 "Look to the Lord and his strength; seek his face always. Remember the wonders he has done, and his miracles…"

Psalm 119:71 "It was good for me to be afflicted so that I might learn your decrees." Through the trials in my life, I can look back and see that my trust and belief in the Lord was strengthened by my afflictions."

Psalm 145:18-19 "The Lord is near to all that call on him, to all who call on him in truth. He fulfills the desires of those who fear him; he hears their cry and saves them."

KANAKUK CHANGES LIVES

JOE WHITE IS THE DIRECTOR OF KANAKUK, A WONDERFUL Christian camp in Missouri, and has dedicated his life's work to leading kids (along with some of their parents) to Christ. I can't impress enough how important it is to send kids to a Christian camp like Kanakuk! *It will change their lives!*

I prayed for months before one of my stepdaughters went to camp for the first time—for her counselors and cabin mates. I asked that she would be open to hear what God had to say to her through Joe and her counselors. As a camper, I loved getting letters and remembered how much it meant to me to receive mail at camp. I wrote her several times a week and sent several packages.

I went to Kanakuk myself for eight years when I was young. It taught me about the Christian life and what it meant to put your faith in Christ. Even though it took many years for these principles to take effect in my life, camp gave me the foundation I needed. Proverbs 22:6 says, "Train a child in the way he should go, and when he is old he will not turn from it." I was off track for years, but when Dad died, I slowly started my journey back to God.

I warned Ben when we went to Missouri to pick her up. "There's a chance I'm gonna cry when we get to camp."

He looked over at me and said, "That's okay. Why do you think that?"

"Because I have so many great memories here. I remember each year where I was when I saw Mom and Dad for the first time when they came to pick me up." I always dropped whatever I was doing and ran as fast as I could to hug them—often wrapping my arms and legs around Dad in a bear hug. (I would have knocked Mom over had I done that to her!)

At camp, I always pushed the limits on what we were supposed to be doing or not doing. You see, I was a rebellious child too. I loved to get into mischief and see just how far I could bend the rules. I was the one who would organize the "short sheeting" of the beds inside the surrounding cabins. We pulled the top sheet up, tucked it into the top of the mattress, and folded the bottom up so it looked like the top sheet. When someone got into bed at night, their legs only went about two feet into the covers! We would also sneak into other cabins and shake baby powder on each blade of the ceiling fan. When the first person came in and flipped the switch, we would all watch the "white out" from our cabin windows. More often than not, I'd hear a loud scream from the other cabins, "Amy!" They knew I'd done it. When I got in trouble, I had to run laps or memorize Bible verses, but it was always worth it.

Sure enough, as we pulled into camp, I cried. As we drove down the long driveway, I pointed out to Ben the different fields where I played soccer, softball, basketball, tennis, and ran track. You name it; I did it. I won the softball throw every year, hands down. I could throw it further than any girl—and most guys. I don't know where that skill came from, but it came in handy when our "tribe" of campers needed points.

As we walked down into the main area of the camp, the memories flooded my mind. I remembered the time I ran full speed to the trampolines and began jumping from one to the other. That was a huge no-no. The rule was "no jumping without a counselor" (and several "spotters" to push you back on the trampoline if you got off balance). Before anyone could stop me, I'd jumped on all four trampolines and then hit the ground running. The ladies in the office saw me and reported it. Another lap around the field. I was always in great shape after camp.

> **As we walked down into the main area of the camp, the memories flooded my mind.**

In the middle of recalling these special memories, I suddenly saw our stepdaughter running up to us and we hugged. She looked happy and introduced us to several friends who were all adorable. We listened to Joe give a talk that night, and the memories surrounded me once again.

"If only they had camp for forty-year-olds," I sighed, thinking to myself. After he finished, I walked up to the mess hall where all the names of the past camp "princesses" were carved on a wooden plaque. Again, more memories. Sue Moore, Maggie Moore, Judy Griffin, Amy Perry… their faces flashed before me as I thought of so many fun times with these girls. Maggie is the only one I keep up with, and we talk once or twice a year. It's sad to be so close your camp buddies, and then when it's over, life goes on. More than likely, the next time I see most of them will be in heaven. However, I'll never forget them.

O n the way home, we kept talking about camp. "So tell me your top three favorite things," I asked her.

She thought for a moment. "Jet skiing, scuba diving, and K-Life."

"Oh, that sounds great! What's K-Life?" I knew what it was, but I wanted to see what she said about it.

"Well, at night the whole camp meets in the gym, and Joe White gives a talk. We sing and they do skits. He did several talks—one on Creation, one on relationships, one on leadership, and one on purity."

I recalled hearing a similar camp talk on Creation many years ago, but I enjoyed hearing about it from her perspective. She explained what she'd learned about how God created the world and universe. "Joe explained that it could *not* be any other way," she said, emphasizing "not." "Darwin's theory had been proven wrong, and the Big Bang Theory doesn't have enough to back itself."

We talked some more, and I could tell that her experience at camp had really impacted her life. When I was a camper, the Holy Spirit moved our hearts in special ways. I know that sounds crazy if you're not a Christian, but when you have experienced that, you will recognize Him immediately. It will bring you to tears, and it's a feeling you can't explain. The closer you come to Christ and begin growing spiritually, you will realize when the Holy Spirit "moves you."

In the car, I had on a Christian radio station I liked. As

we were talking more about camp, she heard the song that was playing on the radio and said, "Oh! That's my new favorite song!" She reached over, turned the volume up, and started singing, "Here I Am to Worship" by Michael W. Smith. And she knew the words! We both started singing the words together. I turned my head to keep her from seeing my tears and pretended as if I were checking the traffic.

We kept singing, and my mind flashbacked to all the months I worried endlessly about her having a good camp experience. God was faithful. He answered my prayers ten-fold. I've never seen a transformation like that in such a short period of time—she was there only two weeks. I felt ashamed for worrying when all along God had heard my prayers. All day, I just kept repeating, "Thank You, Lord."

This story is a huge reminder to me that there is nothing too big for God! He can do anything! He is almighty, all-powerful, and the authority over all.

That night, I recalled how I had felt covered in a peaceful feeling all day. I even wrote Joe an email to thank him. "I know you probably feel this way a lot," I wrote, "but Ben and I are experiencing God's peace and joy in such a way that we can't control our tears. The joy in our hearts is flowing out of us—it is truly amazing! Thank you, Joe, for loving all these kids! Because of your devotion to the Lord, thousands of kids benefit by learning about Jesus Christ and asking Him into their hearts. In such a short time, it transforms their lives!"

Then I thought of all the thousands of parents like me who had prayed for the 15,000 or so children who attend camp over the course of the summer at Kanakuk. God does answer every prayer—all 15,000 of them!

Business Meeting with God

P LAYING TENNIS QUICKLY BECAME A FAVORITE SPORT OF mine. There was a time when I was playing most days of the week, and I ended up joining a TCD (Tennis Competitors of Dallas) team. After years of overhead slams, I began to get tennis elbow. For the most part, I decided to tough it out and just keep swinging. Then the pain became so bad I couldn't squeeze my shampoo bottle, hold a hairbrush, or lift a glass of water to my lips to drink. I fought through that stage, but then the pain increased to the point where it would wake me up in the middle of the night. Something had to be done.

I quit playing and saw a couple of doctors. I tried eight weeks of physical therapy and several other remedies I heard might help. Nothing helped; the only option left was surgery. The kidney transplant was in February, and the trouble with my elbow happened just three months later. My friend, Julie, referred me to a doctor in Vail, Colorado who had fixed a lot of sports celebrity injuries. I told myself that if he was good enough for them, he was good enough for me. His innovative procedure was designed to speed up the recovery. He would take extra blood from my body (ugh) and spin it into a jelly-like substance, then put it back in around the repaired tendon. It sounded promising, so I headed to Vail.

Mom and Harold were supposed to fly to Vail from

Santa Barbara the morning of the surgery (for moral support more than anything). When you're sick or having surgery, we all want our mommies! My surgery was scheduled for 11:00am, and they would arrive just in time. We planned to spend the night in Vail and fly home the next day.

On the morning of the surgery, I woke up about 9:00am. As I sat on the side of the bed, one eye barely open and the other firmly shut, the phone rang. "That's odd," I thought. "Who is calling me now?" I looked at my cell phone and saw it was Mom's number in Santa Barbara where they have a second home. My mind raced..."Wait, shouldn't they be in the air on the way here by now?" I knew something was terribly wrong. I answered, "Mom?"

Her voice was weak and tired. "Hi, Honey...well, we are not going to be able to come today. We just got home from the ER, and we are exhausted.

When you're sick or having surgery, we all want our mommies!

Harold started having problems about 1:00 this morning."

I felt the blood drain down to my feet; I fought back tears. "What's wrong? Is he okay?" All I could think about was getting to Santa Barbara to be there with Mom and Harold. But trying to fly from Vail to Santa Barbara would take all day. I felt stranded and helpless. Mom convinced me that he was fine, but she had to stay there with him. My first thought was to cancel my surgery.

Then Mom said, "Honey, Jimmy and Sue are in Vail. They are going to go to the hospital, sit in the waiting room, and wait for you. Then they will help you get back to the hotel room, too."

I should have known Mom already had a Plan B in place. Her friends, Jimmy Westcott and Sue Justice, were in Vail on vacation. They gladly stepped in to comfort me and play "mom." Also Ben would be there to support me, along with my friend, Rachael, whose mom just happened to have back surgery in the same hospital, on the same day. Coincidence? I don't think so—God knew I needed some extra care and support, since "Mommy" was not going to make it.

When I hung up the phone from Mom, I sat in the Vail hotel room with an incredibly heavy heart. I felt as if I were being "pressed down" by Satan. I was completely overwhelmed with the situation that had evolved in the last three minutes. I walked into the living area and looked up toward heaven. With my hands held high, I yelled, "Okay, Lord, I'm falling apart here. I need You! I need to feel Your peace that You talk about, because I am not doing so well right now!" I'm sure some of our hotel neighbors might have heard me having my "business meeting" with God.

I continued praying, "Please comfort me and replace this feeling with Your peace. Please take care of Harold and Mom, and don't let anything happen to them. Lord, here I am at Your mercy. I need You to help me get through this surgery and this day. Amen." Immediately, I felt so much better—as if a great weight had been lifted from my shoulders. He instantly granted me His peace.

I got dressed and we headed to the hospital. I did quite well, although I dreaded the part where they had to take my blood, which took a long time (30 minutes) because of the procedure to spin the platelets. Ben was beside me every second. He talked to me and held my hand during all the questions, needles, and blood work. Then he kissed me goodbye as they wheeled me off to surgery. I came out 45 minutes later, still under the "goo-goo" juice, as I called the anesthesia. I was so happy!

As promised, Jimmy, Sue, Rachael, and Ben were there for me in the recovery room. I felt extra cozy, snuggled under a fancy hospital blanket that pumped warm air inside it. It was the most comfortable I'd ever been, and I apparently kept telling everyone about it! Recovery is normally an hour or so, but mine was four hours because I was still under the influence of the anesthesia and didn't want to get out of that comfy bed!

About four in the afternoon, they devised a plan to get me out because the hospital needed the bed for another patient. First, they convinced me I needed to go to the bathroom. Ben helped me up and into the bathroom. The plan was to get me dressed meanwhile and replace my bed with a recliner! Ben held me tight as we came out of the bathroom and I discovered my bed was gone!

My eyes grew wide and I announced, "We're not in the right room!"

"Yes we are. They just needed your bed, so they took it out."

In my "goo-goo" juiced state, I insisted we were definitely in the wrong room. To keep me quiet, they brought back the heated blanket that I had fallen in love with and coaxed me to sit in the recliner by draping the blanket over me.

Sue, Jimmy, and Rachael had been there all day with me, and when I was finally ready to go back to the hotel it was quite a precession. Ben led the way with my bags, Jimmy pushed me in the wheelchair, Sue followed close behind with huge beautiful flowers, and Rachael parked the car. I'm sure people thought I'd been in the hospital for days! We got up to the hotel room, and the girls helped Ben get me settled. I talked to Mom but don't remember telling her much except that "I was the most comfortable I'd ever been."

This story might seem like no big deal to you. *So my mom couldn't come to be with me during my elbow surgery—big deal, right?* Well, it was a big deal to me. My mom and I are so close—I want her beside me even if it's to pull out a splinter! (Which she has done many times!) Going through the surgery without Mom and Harold there with me was one thing. But knowing Harold was not doing well on the day I was having surgery added a whole other level of stress and anxiety.

The point of my story is that in the midst of my despair, I called out (or yelled, in this case) to God, and He answered my prayers that instant. I knew I could trust Him, based on my previous experiences with Him. And He gave me perfect peace. He relieved all the pain and angst about my situation. God doesn't say He will change our situations, but He does say He will give us peace *in the middle* of our trials. He did that for me during this particular trial. When I gave it to God, He answered my prayers and lifted my burdens immediately.

Harold, and me the day after the kidney
transplant. It was the first time to see each other.

Mom, me, Harold, and my brother Andy,
walking the halls at Baylor Hospital.

This is Harold and me on our first walk,
unassisted, hand in hand.

Harold and me,
one month after the
transplant. Mom had
a party "celebrating
life." Twenty men
sang gospel songs
while walking
through the crowd.

It was a day I'll never forget!

Buster and me on a
Saturday afternoon
ride at the farm
where he was later
buried.

He LOVED the farm.

Buster's grave, overlooking our family farm
in McKinney, Texas.

Buddy. Funny how much both dogs loved
riding 4-wheelers with me!

Buddy and Buster in their monogrammed
raincoats so we know whose is whose!

President George Bush and me in the
Diplomat Room in the White House.

Exactly five weeks
after the kidney
transplant.

...anding in front
...he Oval Office.
...hy, Susan, Paige,
...e, and Rachael.

We had a private tour of the West Wing.

Just another day at the farm! 18 years old, and I was just getting started!

It's absolutely beautiful up there.

This was my fourth time up Aspen Mountain. I love being 13,000 feet closer to God!

The morning after the Tea Fire where our next door neighbor lost everything.

am dousing the flames still burning in the rubble.

e squiggly lights are a line of retrucks fighting the fire.

I took this photo of the Tea Fire just 50 feet from the wall in our yard.

Paige, me, Jackie, and Chantell in Paris, France.
Bon Jour!

Trying to navigate our way through Paris.

My niece, Little A, and me in front of the Dome of the Rock, made of gold!

The building is beautifully colored with tiny mosaic tiles.

's part of the wall there in Jesus' day.

Me praying for my niece, Little A, at the "Wailing Wall."

I think about what it is was like for the disciples to see Jesus walking on the water on this very lake.

The Sea of Galilee, so peaceful and pretty.

Celebrating my birthday and the 2 1/2 year anniversary of the kidney transplant!

Me, Harold, and Mom in the San Juan islands

When God Intervenes in MINISTRY

MY FIRST PRISON MINISTRY EXPERIENCE

I HAD ALWAYS WANTED TO VISIT A PRISON. FOR SOME reason, God had put that on my heart. And not just any prison. If I got the chance, I wanted to visit a maximum-security prison where they house the worst of the worst inside.

I wrote about my introduction to prison ministry in my first book, *When God Has a Way No Other Way Works*, and this is the rest of the story! I went to my first prison with a group of 15 people I did not know. However, I got my wish—we were going inside a female prison where the worst of the worst murderers and criminals are spending life sentences.

On December 22, the night before our trip, I got a taste of what it feels like to be "hit on" by the evil one. (I don't even like to acknowledge Satan's name, so I call him "the evil one"). After years of wanting to do prison ministry, I started to have doubts. For one thing, we were supposed to leave at five o'clock Sunday morning (which wipes out any Saturday night plans). The night before, I was beginning to dread how early I would have to get up.

Then I started wondering if it would be worth my while. What if I couldn't talk to the inmates one-on-one? I wanted to share the Gospel with one or two girls and "save" someone in the prison unit. But something made me doubt that I would even get that chance.

So, I began to figure out a way to get out of going—starting with the fact that I didn't want to get up at four o'clock! I decided to call the pastor of Cornerstone Ministries to see if they really needed me.

The phone rang twice before a woman answered.

"Hello?"

"Is Chaplain Gibbons there?" I asked.

"Who's this?" she said in a friendly voice.

"Um, this is Amy Alford…I'm supposed to go with you tomorrow to the Murray Unit but…"

Before I could offer my excuse, she said, "Oh Amy, it's so nice to talk to you, I've heard so much about you, and I'm looking so forward to meeting you tomorrow!"

Oh, great. "Oh, okay." My mind was racing. "Are we going to be able to talk to the girls one-on-one?" I asked. I told myself if I couldn't talk or witness to the girls one-on-one, I might as well stay at home.

"Oh no, Honey. We just pass out 'blessing bags,' have a chapel service, and then we come home. We are so glad you're coming tomorrow!"

I still wanted to back out, but I knew there was no way I could do it now! So I just said, "Great, see you tomorrow" and hung up the phone.

Looking back on that night and that conversation, I realize the "evil one" was working on me. After everything that happened at the prison unit, it's no wonder he put doubtful thoughts in my head to discourage me from going! Now I see his strategy, but at the time I was just making logical excuses not to go.

∞

Despite my doubts, I woke up at four o'clock the next morning and got going. Even after a long van ride down together from Dallas to the Gatesville prison, I still didn't know anyone in my group very well. So, when we entered the prison, I started striking up conversations and trying to get to know some of the female prisoners. It was Christmastime and a chilly 38 degrees outside as we handed out care packages called "blessing bags."

Inside the prison yard, one of the prisoners I'd befriended pointed out another prisoner with shackles who was being escorted by two huge men. This highly visible prisoner had murdered the well-known Hispanic recording artist, Selena. My new friend explained she was under the guards' protection so the other inmates wouldn't harm her!

The security at a maximum-security prison is extraordinarily tight. For example, can you tell the difference between a maximum and minimum-security prison when you drive by? I can now. The maximum-security prison has two rolls of razor wire on top of the fence, while the minimum-security prisons have only one. We gave our drivers licenses at the front office when we arrived, but we had already been thoroughly checked out weeks ahead of time. All visitors are brought into a gated area that has a literal cage. Both the entrance and exit gates lock for a minute or so before the visitors are allowed to pass through to the next section. We went through several secure checkpoints like that before we actually entered the prison yard to pass out our care packages. To say I felt unsafe and afraid in this environment is more than an understatement. I was in a maximum-security prison, virtually on my own.

Luckily, the girls were glad to see us.

After we passed out 1500 bags, our group went into town for lunch, planning to return to the prison later that afternoon. The Texas metropolis of Gatesville has only three fast food restaurants, and Dairy Queen won the popular vote among my group. I followed along like a lost puppy, ordered a basket of greasy steak fingers and sat down with the strangers in my group. My lunch was barely edible, but I found that with enough gravy, I was able to get a few pieces down. I could tell this group had been in prison ministry together for many years, and it was evident they all knew each other well.

They were from the same town, but they had never seen me before in their lives. I looked around and realized how easy it would be for them to accidentally leave me and never miss me until hours later. As they talked and told stories, I intervened at one point and said (only half-jokingly), "No matter what happens today, don't leave me!" They laughed and went back to their "Belt Buster" hamburgers and fries. Not certain I'd been convincing enough, I made my point again to the van driver and his wife, "Please, please do not leave me."

You may think I sounded paranoid, but I have this thing—it's like a hunch or premonition where I often know something's going to happen long before it does. Whatever you call it, I'm right about 70% of the time. After lunch, we got back in the van and returned to the prison just in time to lead a church service for the prisoners. Again, I had no idea this was part of their routine, but I just followed my group from one activity to the next.

As the 15 people in our group squeezed back into

the "cage" again waiting to be buzzed in, the chaplain said, "Does anyone want to give their testimony during the church service?" No one wanted to make eye contact with him. They either looked down or around, and an awkward silence followed for about 10 seconds. I thought to myself, "I'll say something. What do I have to lose? I'll never see any of these people again." (Or so I thought—remember, God had something else in mind.) I broke the silence and piped up, "I'll say something." Instead of being pleased, the chaplain retorted, "Well, you can't just say *something*...you gotta give your testimony."

I'd never given my testimony in my life. I didn't even know what my "testimony" was. *What would I say?*

Without hesitating, I replied, "Okay, I'll give my testimony." Even as I heard the words come out of my mouth, I thought to myself, *Who just said that? Did I just volunteer to do it?* Any chance I had to change my mind was interrupted by the loud, long "buzzzz" of the gate releasing us into the prison yard. I had a 400-yard walk down the middle of the yard toward the chapel to think of my testimony. We had to walk single file down a marked path, escorted by armed guards. I prayed repeatedly, "Lord, put Your words in my mouth. Let them hear You when I speak, because this is Your deal!" I asked Him to open their hearts to hear Him through me.

> I thought to myself, "I'll say something. What do I have to lose?"

The chapel was full with about 400 prisoners. The day before, I'd pictured sharing the Gospel with one or two girls. But God had a different plan, and His plans are so much better than our own!

While we sang worship music, I was frantically looking up scripture verses in my Bible, hoping to find something they could relate to. Before I knew it, I heard the chaplain on the microphone say, "We'd like to call up sister Amy to come speak to you."

I froze. "Let's welcome Amy."

My heart was beating hard enough to make my sweater bounce. I slowly walked up to the stage and stood in front of the microphone to address the women— all dressed in white, all eyes on me. The walls were lined with armed guards. "Okay, Lord," I whispered, "showtime." I hope He "showed" up, because I had never done anything like this before!

Fifteen minutes later, I had finished. I don't remember much except my voice wasn't shaking, and I no longer felt nervous at all. At one point, they were crying, then laughing, then praising God. The last thing I said was, "Remember this: How can you stumble when you're on your knees?" As I walked off the stage and down the aisle next to the armed guards, the prisoners on the edge of the rows were high fivin' me and clapping and cheering. I took my seat on the back row, amazed that my knees did not shake. It was as if my body had been up there on stage, but God had taken control of my words. He used me as His vessel and spoke through me—just exactly as I had prayed.

While the service continued, several young prisoners came over to me. They knelt down on the floor as if not to be seen and said, "We loved what you said…can you go back up and keep talking? We need more people like you to talk to us." That's when I realized they related to younger people and thought of me as closer to their age. (I have to admit, I enjoy a sense of humor and use it every chance I get. They obviously appreciated it in my talk.) I felt honored that so many of the girls felt a connection with me.

I give the glory to God. He's the one who made that happen. It was His doing, not mine. I would never take the credit—especially when I didn't want to go in the first place! I was simply obedient and available for His purpose, and it was obvious He planned to draw them to Christ through the stories He placed on my heart to tell them.

As the worship service came to an end, the girls began filing out in an orderly manner, but some gathered around me. One girl called out, "Hey Amy! I love your hair...I'm going to get mine cut like yours!"

I admit, my first thought was, *Who's going to cut it? Can they have scissors in here?* Several girls told me their story. They asked me to pray for them. I held their hands or put my arm around them (knowing they don't get hugs because it's against prison rules to touch or be affectionate to each other). I was completely caught up in the moment, seeing God at work with these precious girls. Next thing I knew, one of the inmates looked around and said, "Amy, your group left you."

"What?" I tried not to sound startled. "Oh, I'm sure they're just out in the hallway."

"No, they're gone," was the consensus. They were right!

I quickly wrapped up my visit with the girls, grabbed my Bible and coat, and headed into the hallway. No one from my group was there. I dashed out into the 38-degree weather and made my way through the first few gates into the prison yard, all alone. My group was nowhere to be seen. About 400 yards away, I happened to see them entering the last set of gates. I took off running as if I were making a break for it out of this place! I ran down the middle of the prison yard, weaving through all the prisoners. Some of them waved and said, "Bye, Amy! God bless you!" I was calling out *God bless you* here and there, trying to smile and not reveal my sheer panic. It was getting dark by now, and the cold air stung my throat and inside of my chest. I had not run that fast since my eighth grade track meet. I was 100 yards from the last gate when I met eyes with an armed guard. She had this crazy white woman running across the prison yard in her sights.

That's when I began screaming and waving my arms saying, "Wait, wait! I'm with them!" My group had passed through the last secure area and was now headed inside the building. The guard had one hand on her gun and one on the gate. I was completely out of gas but determined not to be locked in with some pretty tough ladies (to put it nicely). I was frantic now, and I knew it showed on my red, cold face as I ran the last 50 yards. As I approached the guard, she said without the slightest hint of humor, "If you were wearing white, you would have been shot." That was the least of my worries!

Finally, I came through the home stretch inside the building and yelled one last time at my group. They nonchalantly turned to see what all the commotion was. I was doubled over trying to catch my breath, and when I did, I managed to heave out, "I…told you…not…to…leave…me." One of the ladies just smiled and said, "Oh, we're sorry. We thought you were with us." I'm now a firm believer in the buddy system.

It's hard to explain the feeling I had on the way home. I forgot all about almost being left in prison! I burst through the back door of my house and yelled out to Ben. My adrenaline was still pounding with joy—a joy that can only come straight from God. It was such an awesome feeling, and Ben was so thrilled for me. He could feel the joy radiating from the inside out. Have you ever had a similar feeling when God seemed to pour His joy over you?

> **I took off running as if I were making a break for it out of this place!**

I had experienced being in God's will, and I saw the results of my obedience to Him. Remember, my original plan was to try and talk to one or two inmates. However, God allowed me to speak to many more. In fact, 22 girls came to Christ that day after hearing my testimony and listening to the chaplain's talk. Twenty-two! It wasn't the experience I had planned (talking to one or two girls), but I'm so glad that God worked His plan in my life instead.

He proved to me once again that He is in control. If we are open and available to Him, He will work His purposes through us. His will *is* far better than ours. Because I was available and compliant with God's will, He used me to lead so many to Him. It's true—when God has a way, no other way works!

BLESSED TO BE A BLESSING

AFTER MY FIRST EXPERIENCE WITH PRISON MINISTRY, I knew it would not be my last. In fact, my friend, Mary Beth Gaylor, and I decided to make a monthly visit to Dawson State Jail in downtown Dallas. On our visits, we usually went from dorm to dorm to distribute Christian books for the inmates to read. I felt led to donate about 60 copies of my first book to the jail, unsure if anyone would read them or not.

One day Mary Beth and I were in the lockdown area waiting to be "buzzed" into the dorms. As we entered, one of the girls seemed to be looking closely at me. Then her eyes grew as big as dinner plates as she exclaimed, "Are you the one on the cover of that book?"

She was obviously referring to one of the books I'd donated, which happens to have a picture of me on the cover walking together in a garden with my mentor, Sandy. Mary Beth giggled under her breath at the stunned look on my face, which she later deemed "priceless." I'd never had that kind of reaction to my book before. Not knowing what else to say to the young woman, I smiled kindly and agreed, "Yes, I am! What's your name?"

"Mary Ann," she said. "My mama is a reverend in Virginia, and I've been writing her and telling her about the things in your book. She sometimes uses what you wrote to preach her sermons on Sundays!"

That made me feel so good to know my book had helped at least two people! I got Mary Ann's and her mom's address that day and sent autographed books to both of them. Soon after, I received a four-page typed letter from her mom thanking me. I then called her mom to thank her for telling me what a difference the principles I'd learned from Sandy had made in Mary Ann's life.

Another friend also told me a great story about someone who was touched by the book. Jackie, my Tyler friend whose dad was undergoing cancer treatment, called one day and said, "I have the neatest story to tell you. While my dad was waiting for his radiation treatment, he was reading your book. A nurse saw the book in his hands, stopped and said, 'Oh my gosh... that's the best book I've ever read!'"

Now, who knows if it was really the best book she's ever read? But still, little stories like that amaze me. Not because of anything I've done—but because of how God can intervene and use anything when we step out in faith for Him.

Another time, two ladies from Sandy's Bible class were at the Dallas Museum of Art. In their conversation with the docent, they discovered the girl was a Christian. After spending some time walking around with them in the museum, the docent revealed that she was going through a bad divorce. She then mentioned a book she'd read that had helped her through tough times. Guess what book it was? You got it.

I recently read a devotional about how we can be a blessing to someone every day. The verse was Romans 1:11, which says, "I long to see you so that I may impart to you some spiritual gift to make you strong..." Paul wanted to be a blessing to other people, so he wrote them a letter of encouragement. You do not need to have written a book to help someone. A few years ago, I'd never written a book before in my life! You don't need to know all the right Bible verses or be a theologian to attract others to the Lord. It's the way we act that gets their attention. (Let me make it clear—I don't always act like Christ. And I know it! But it is something I strive for every day.) You might not realize it, but your life has the potential to bless everyone you meet—even strangers like the ones I mentioned in this story. Your life is the "book" that people around you read every day. When you enter a room, how do others see you? Are you the life of the party? Do you bring others down? Or do people see Jesus in you? Remember, you are blessed in order to be a blessing to those around you every day.

A PRIVATE MEETING WITH THE PRESIDENT

WHEN I WAS AT HOME RECOVERING FROM MY kidney surgery, my friends Rachael and Bob Dedman and Kathy Wills Wright came over to visit and bring me dinner. I met Rachael about 16 years ago in a Bible study and her close friend, Kathy, shortly after that. Kathy and Rachael were fortunate enough to work in the White House, and they still have ties with a lot of people there. As I was telling them about my surgery, Kathy remarked, "Wow, you have an incredible story. Would you consider coming to the White House to speak about your book and tell your kidney story?"

I couldn't believe it, and I immediately agreed to go. I'd only driven by the White House a few times—I'd never actually been inside. And, at the time, I'd only spoken once in public at the prison chapel service. But I just told myself it wouldn't be too much different from the prison. We would be surrounded with guards, only the audience wouldn't be dressed in white this time! Within a couple of weeks, "Robert" contacted me from the White House, and we set the date for April 8.

You might not realize it, but your life has the potential to bless everyone you meet.

Kathy arranged for me to bring Rachael and Paige with me to the White House. My dear friend, Susan Pausky, lives in D.C. and was able to come as well. Robert and I had several phone calls to coordinate the details. During one of our conversations, he said, "I'm going to try to do something special for you. It's a really neat thing to watch the President take off in Marine One from the south lawn. He is scheduled to leave about 10:00 the morning you arrive."

"Oh, do you know where he is going?" I asked him. Silence.

"No…" he said cautiously, not wanting to reveal the President's whereabouts.

"I do," I replied matter-of-factly. About this time, I bet Robert was thinking, "Uh, oh! Security breach!"

"How do you know that?" he asked, curious to see what I'd say.

"He is going to his Crawford ranch to have lunch with my parents." More silence.

"Who are your parents?"

"Annette and Harold."

"Can I call you back?" Robert hung up the phone.

I think he freaked out because I knew where the President was going. My mom had already told me they were going to Crawford to have lunch with George and Laura the day I was to speak in Washington. I didn't think it would be a big deal if I told Robert about the President's lunch plans. Robert called back within the next few days (satisfied that I was no longer a security threat I guess!), and we continued planning the "White House Ministries" speaking engagement.

Paige, Rachael, and I flew out the day before and stayed at a hotel near the White House. We took Kathy to dinner that night and told stories from our college days. That brought back lots of memories. We laughed so hard we might have disturbed the others around us, but we had a great time.

The next morning, I woke up praying and practicing my speech. We were scheduled to arrive at the White House by 9:30am, and I would speak at 11:00. A driver picked us up at the hotel to take us to the White House. On the way there, I said, "Let's say a prayer before we get there." The three of us bowed our heads and held hands in the backseat. "Dear Lord," I began, "thank You for this opportunity to speak to the staff at the White House. Lord, please speak though me so that they can understand what You want to say through me. Open their hearts so they can hear You. Please give me peace and remove any nervousness I feel. This is Your day and Your body that You've given me. Please use me to glorify You. Amen."

Kathy and Susan met us at the West Wing entrance. Security was tight. We received special nametags that gave us certain security clearance. Robert also met us there and Kathy introduced us, although I felt as if I already knew him because of all our phone calls. He was young, slender, and handsome with a great smile. He and Kathy gave us a tour of the West Wing. Kathy knew everybody by name: every policeman, every secret service person, everyone we passed.

We went to the dining room where all the commissioned officers of the White House can eat. The china had a picture of the Presidential seal on it. The photographs that lined the halls were incredible, including a lot of candid shots of the President. One of my favorites was of him and his dog looking at each other at what appeared to be the Crawford ranch. The President was wearing blue jeans and boots, and he was sitting on a wooden bench outside. Another photo of him was at Ground Zero right after 9-11. One of the most moving photographs for me was a picture of Marine One flying over a town that had just been hit by a tornado. You could see the path of destruction winding through the town in the background. Every photograph told a story, and, being a photographer, I loved each one.

Next, we walked past the Oval Office, but we could not go in. The doors were shut, and Robert said there was a meeting going on inside. My mind raced as I thought of all the people who had been there, served there, and lived there. Robert had said there were certain areas where we could not take photos, so I complied (for the most part). My friends and I did take our own photograph in front of the Presidential seal in the West Wing. That was fun! At the end of our tour, we came out into the Rose Garden, the area right outside the Oval Office that I've seen a million times on TV when the President addresses the nation. As we walked along the outside corridor, I held up my pocket-sized camera and just started snapping pictures as we walked along—without even looking through the lens. Now I know where they get the expression "point and shoot."

We walked by the Garden and onto the South Lawn where a few hundred people waited behind a roped-off area. We were standing near the door below all the big white columns, another part of the White House you've likely seen on TV. However, we were not behind the ropes with everyone else. As we stood there waiting, Paige and I could hardly stop smiling. The White House staff did this all the time, and they were used to being at the White House. But we were so excited to be there and see everything in person. As we looked around from our prime spot, Robert suddenly tapped me on the shoulder and said, "Mrs. Alford, you can come with me."

All I could think about was how the surveillance

camera must have caught me shooting photos as we walked along the Rose Garden. I thought I was in big trouble. We walked into the main door into the White House and stood in the Diplomat Room, a large, oval-shaped room. It was blue and yellow and had a fireplace with a portrait of George Washington hanging above the mantel.

"Wow," I thought silently. *Oh wait, am I in trouble?* I still wasn't sure.

We stopped in the middle of the room. Robert had a clipboard in his hand with the President's itinerary on it, containing minute-by-minute details of where he was to be.

"I didn't want to tell you this ahead of time because the President's schedule changes so quickly," Robert explained. "He is upstairs right now in the Blue Room addressing the nation on the war in Iraq. When he finishes, he wants to come down here and meet you."

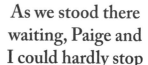

As we stood there waiting, Paige and I could hardly stop smiling.

Whew. I wasn't in trouble after all! "Meet me? What do I say? How do I address him?" My questions tumbled out all together. "Do I call him George? Mr. Bush? Mr. President? I photographed him when he was Governor, and he said to call him 'George.'"

Robert just smiled patiently and replied, "You need to call him Mr. President. I need to inform you of what will happen when he arrives. About 15-20 Secret Service men will enter the room. They will do a quick check around as the President is walking in. It's rather weird, but they will walk out of the room backwards, almost like a vacuum has sucked them out. Then a photographer will come in and take several photos of you. I'm guessing you'll have about one to two minutes with him before he leaves on Marine One, exiting out the same door that you came in. Any questions?"

"Where will you be?" I asked.

"I will be in the hall with the Secret Service," Robert replied.

"Okay, I think I got it. Can you snap a photo of us before you leave?" I asked.

"I'll try, but I'm not sure if I can." I was still thinking about his answer when a lady came walking through the room carrying a duffle bag in each hand. She was moving pretty quickly. Robert said to her, "Hey Janet. I see you're carrying the football."

"Yes," she replied, not even slowing down.

"That's such a privilege and honor," Robert called after her.

"Oh, I know!' said Janet, but she never missed a step. "I'm loving my job." And she was gone.

"What's the football?" I asked, wondering what was inside those bags.

"Those bags she is carrying," Robert explained, "hold the detonating device and codes in case we are attacked with nuclear bombs. She always travels with the President. I would have tried to get her to slow down and talk to us, but she's not allowed to stop." I was amazed by everything I was seeing, and the President wasn't even here yet!

Next, we walked in the China Room, containing rows and rows of beautiful china plates from all over the world, all neatly displayed on lighted shelves. The room was red with a sitting area in the middle. After I gazed at all the china, I had Robert take a picture in front of the fireplace with the George Washington portrait behind me. He told me he wanted one, too; he'd never been in the Diplomat Room.

Then we walked into the main hallway, and I saw a couple of Secret Service men standing guard. They had on suits, hands folded together in front, and they were wearing earpieces with the telephone cord coming from behind one ear. We ducked back into the Diplomat Room, and just a few moments later I heard the sound of a herd of feet coming quickly down the hall. I thought, "Is that him?" Just then Robert said, "Here comes the President!"

At once, Robert leaped over the ottoman, striding toward the door. I was left standing in the middle of the room. I whispered loudly, "Here, take my picture" and literally threw him my camera. Luckily, he caught it just as the Secret Service rounded the corner.

I flipped my hair, straightened my vest, and stood at attention. I was ready to meet the most powerful man in the world, the President of the United States, George W. Bush. And as he came around the corner, he greeted me with, "Hi Amy! How ya doin'?"

"Good, Mr. President. How are you?" I didn't know what else to say.

"Good, let's get a picture." I looked around. The human vacuum came and started sucking out all the Secret Service, just as Robert had said. We took several pictures. I am not used to being on that side of the camera, so I was trying to give my best "Here I am with the President" smile. By the time the photography session was over, so was the vacuum.

"Let's have a seat," he offered and held out his arms toward the big, yellow, wing-backed chairs in front of the fireplace. He was so relaxed and easy-going. There was a small round table between the chairs, but we were sitting so close I had to be careful not to kick him when I crossed my feet. "What are you doing here?" he asked.

"I am speaking to your staff in the Bible class," I replied.

He nodded. "Which one?"

Oh my gosh, there is more than one Bible class? I said, "All I know is it's called the White House Ministries."

"What are you speaking on?" he wanted to know.

"My book that I wrote." I didn't think to tell him the title!

"What's the name of it?" he leaned back in the chair, so relaxed.

I told him the title and a little bit about the book. "That sounds like a good book," he said. *The President just said my book sounded good!*

"Well, I hope it will encourage and inspire people," I said. "I hear you are having lunch with my parents tomorrow."

"Laura and I are looking forward to it. Say, how's your dad? Last time I talked to him, he was needing a kidney transplant."

I told him Harold had undergone surgery five weeks ago and was doing great.

"Where did he find the kidney?"

I told him I gave him mine.

"What? You're the donor?" He sat up from his initial

relaxed position and looked at me from head to toe as if surprised to see me doing so well. "You're the donor!" He couldn't believe it. "How are you doing?"

"I'm great," I said, smiling. "A tiny bit weak, but other than that, I'm good."

"What a generous, kind act…what a blessing you are to him. I'm so impressed, what a selfless act. And he is good?"

"He's great—working, playing golf. He's so much better."

"What a special person you are to do that," he added. "That's amazing."

I was ready to get the attention off of me, to be honest. So I told him, "I just wanted to tell you that I pray for you and Laura every single day. I pray the Lord will guide you in every decision you make, and I know you have to make some tough ones.

⤸

> **"You know, there are people praying for me that I've never met,"** he said humbly.

He said that meant a lot to him. "You know, there are people praying for me that I've never met," he said humbly.

"You have no idea!" I said. (I know a lot of people who pray for him.) "It is an honor and a privilege to pray for you, and it makes me feel good to know that you are a Believer and to know our President is being guided by the Lord. It is a comfort to me knowing you have probably prayed about every decision you make."

Then I told him about a time I was in a restaurant in the Adirondack Mountains with my parents after 9-11.

I remember the entire place grew quiet when he came on TV to address the nation. I recalled how he quoted Psalm 23: "Even though I walk through the valley of the shadow of death, I will fear no evil, for you are with me, your rod and your staff, they comfort me."

"I don't know how I would do it without Him," he assured me. We talked about a lot of things, including the George Bush Library at SMU in Dallas. He is a genuinely nice, easy-to-be-with, humble president, and he has a great sense of humor as well! Our little get-together lasted almost 20 minutes.

As we said our goodbyes, Marine One was landing outside. He gave me some M&M's that said "The White House" on them, and as he was leaving, he said, "You want to watch me take off?"

"Yes, I'd love to!" and he motioned me outside with him.

As soon as he hit the door, I could hear the crowd cheering and clapping. He began to wave to everyone, and I saw my friends standing there. I'm sure Paige was doing some kind of cheerleading move as he walked by. I heard him say, "Hi girls," as he looked back over his shoulder at me and said, "Are these your friends?"

"Yes!" I replied, hoping Paige had not fainted in the pathway from excitement.

I walked about one step behind the President, waving from side to side as if I were part of the show. I did not follow him all the way out to Marine One, but I was tempted. The departure was indeed quite a sight. I remember the loud humming noise of the engine, the swirling wind around the blades, and the President waving goodbye out the window. They shot off like a cannon out of sight, with the Washington Monument in the background.

My friends were thrilled—our feet were barely touching the ground! Wow, what a day already—and I had not even addressed the White House staff yet. We walked back through the Rose Garden, noting the cherry blossoms blooming. Once again, we stopped and Robert took photos of us with the doors to the Oval Office in the background. I guess that was no longer a security breach after all!

Then we all filed into a large conference room where several of the staff were waiting to hear me speak. It was now almost 11:00, which was perfect because Sandy was teaching Bible class at exactly that time back in Texas. I knew they would all stop and pray for me during the time I was to speak. As I pulled out a chair to sit down, I thought, "Sandy and the class are praying right now for me. That must be why I am not shaking." I felt the same sense of total peace I had when I shared my testimony at the prison. Robert introduced me as a photographer and author and mentioned the famous people I have had the privilege to photograph over the years. It was rather strange listening to someone else speak of my accomplishments and what I've done in my life. I almost felt as if I were at my own funeral.

As Robert finished his introduction, he turned to me and said, "May I introduce Mrs. Amy Alford." *Okay, God, You're up.* I spoke to the group about the things in my life that have strengthened and developed my relationship with the Lord. I told them about how my dad, Larry, had died from cancer at an early age (fifty-seven) and how it was his death that began my walk with the Lord. It took something so devastating like my dad's death to get me on the right track. I said how it felt as if I had a direct connection with heaven, now that my dad was there. Knowing your dad is in the *presence of the Lord* is amazing.

My heart was broken at the time, but I told the people in that conference room how God granted me peace and joy during my crisis. Just knowing Dad was safe in heaven, his body instantly restored, was a relief. I know there is no more pain or suffering, only happiness and joy for him as he stands before the Lord. Even though tears stream down my face whenever I think of him, I also have a smile because I know I will see him again.

His death got me thinking about a question. "What would happen if I died at fifty-seven?" I decided I better shape up and start living the life God intended me to live. *But what does that look like?* I wasn't sure. I started by getting involved in as many Bible studies as I could. I was able to keep up with four a week, and I was excited about each one, each week. I began to learn and grow quickly in my faith, and I desired to learn all I could about Jesus and His will for me.

I told the White House Staff about the Bible classes I did, including *Experiencing God* by Henry Blackaby, several studies by Beth Moore and *The Purpose Driven Life*. I love that book! Reading it inspired me to serve others on mission trips and in prison ministry. Those experiences opened my eyes and heart to a whole new level of compassion, love, and caring. I finished my talk by sharing about how leading people to Christ not only changes their life; it changes yours, too.

God tells us we all have a purpose. We are here for several reasons but mainly to tell others about Christ. Jesus said, "Therefore, go and make disciples of all nations... teaching them to obey everything I have commanded you. And surely I am with you always, to the very end of the age," (Matthew 28:19-20). In other words, we are responsible for telling our kids and grandkids about Jesus Christ and salvation. We are held responsible for each generation that follows us, so that they too will know about Jesus and His sacrificial death on the cross for us.

Psalm 22:30-31 says, "Posterity will serve him; future generations will be told about the Lord. They will proclaim his righteousness

> **It took something so devastating like my dad's death to get me on the right track.**

to a people yet unborn—for he has done it." Our faithfulness today matters to tomorrow's generation of men and women. If we fail to do our part and share about Christ with others, especially in our own families, we disrupt the influence God wants us to have on future generations. The Bible says in Proverbs 22:6, "Train a child in the way he should go, and when he is old he will not turn from it." I'm so glad God gave me the opportunity to have some influence, however large or small, on the men and women who were helping shape our country's future.

After I finished my talk, we had a "Q&A" session. My

friend, Susan Pausky, asked, "How has your relationship been with Harold since the kidney transplant?" I told her we'd always had a good relationship, but now we have a special bond. I've always loved him, but this is one way I was able to show him how much, and I would do it all over again if necessary.

Harold has been so sweet to me and done so many things for me that I could never repay. "But I think I'm good for a couple of Christmases!" I joked and everyone laughed. I answered a few more questions, then signed books for the people there. The entire day was something out of a movie; it was a once-in-a-lifetime opportunity, and I'm so blessed and honored. Thank you to everyone for making it possible!

When God Intervenes in
CRISIS

NEAR TRAGEDY IN
THE TEA FIRE

IN THE FALL OF 2008, MOM AND HAROLD ASKED IF I wanted to come to Santa Barbara with them for a long weekend at their second home in the foothills of Montecito. I invited my good friend, Beth Montgomery, to go with me on this quick getaway since she'd never been to my parents' house.

Santa Barbara holds a special place in my heart. During my freshman year of college, I took a photography class and watched amazed as my first photo "came to life" in the dark room. I ran outside the room and announced to my professor, "This is what I want to do the rest of my life! What do I need to do now?" He said if I was serious, I needed to go to Brooks Photography Institute in Santa Barbara, the best school for photography.

"Where's that?" I asked, mentally picturing a map of the United States.

"California." Big smile. I was hooked. I called Brooks that day for a brochure and was thrilled to discover the college had three campuses in the area. One was in Montecito (the Beverly Hills of Santa Barbara), and the other two were on the Riviera overlooking Santa Barbara, the harbor, the beach, and the Anacapa Islands. In my opinion, this area is one of the top five most beautiful places in the country.

Next, I called my mother back home and told her I'd figured out what I want to do as a career. She agreed to talk to Harold about flying out there for a visit soon. When we went to Santa Barbara in the summer of 1985 to check out Brooks, Mom and Harold fell in love with Montecito, a small suburb nestled in the mountains above the city! They even ended up buying Piranhurst from Gene Hackman (the actor)—a 1914 estate home and one of the oldest homes in the area. "Perfect!" I thought to myself. "Now I have a place to live while I'm in photography school!"

This area at the top of the Santa Ynez Mountains has an interesting history. In 1895, a man named Henry Bothin bought 325 acres in Montecito and built his dream home at the lower part of the mountain. He named it "Piranhurst" after St. Piran, an Irish saint. "Piranhurst," along with the Bothin name, is chiseled into the stone at the entrance of the property, which is shaped like a vertical rectangle.

The house itself is tucked into the back of the property, with a guesthouse 60 yards from the back gate and fence. A small road runs between the back wall of my parents' property and the rest of the land that is called the Tea House property. My mom loves roses, and one of her most favorite things to do is taking a walk through the rose gardens surrounding the house. She'll cut some beautiful displays of flowers and roses to arrange in vases and place them throughout the house. The roses grow really big in California, some as big as footballs. The property is truly a paradise, and it might even give the Garden of Eden a run for its money!

Mr. Bothin's wife built a "tea house" at the top of the mountain, overlooking their home and providing a beautiful 180-degree view of land and sea. She named the Tea House "Mar Y Cel," the Catalan Spanish translation of "Sea and Sky." She and her friends would spend afternoons at the Tea House enjoying the incredible view of the beach, islands, and ocean. Sometimes when I'm up there with friends, I'll tease and say, "On a really clear day, you can see Maui."

Over the years, the property was split into two pieces. My parents bought the 25-acre piece with Piranhurst and the guesthouse; the rest of the property

is mountainous terrain, topped by the Tea House, which is still there today in the middle of 300 underdeveloped acres. I often think of the Bothins and their vision to build this glorious place almost 100

The roses grow really big in California, some as big as footballs.

years ago. This beautiful property and home had withstood earthquakes, fires, and floods over the years, but on that fateful visit we made in 2008, it was about to be tested once again.

The four of us arrived in Santa Barbara later than normal because Sandy and I had just completed our first radio interview about my first book, *When God Has A Way, No Other Way Works*. As soon as the interview was over, I jumped on the plane and headed out. Beth and I unpacked all our things in the guesthouse, and then we went to the main house to watch the sunset. Mom placed her roses in arrangements while Harold, Beth, and I sat on the front porch looking out over the ocean. Harold was telling Beth all about the house and its history when I smelled what I thought was pinion wood burning. The Santa Ana winds had stirred up about 30 minutes after we arrived—very strong winds (up to 70mph) that come from the desert, up over the mountain, and down to the ocean. These bursts of hot air are sometimes very frightening because they are so strong.

I couldn't believe someone was having a fire in those winds. I continued to smell smoke and walked out to the end of the porch. I looked around and didn't see anything, so I sat back down with Beth and Harold. Just then, I saw one fire truck drive past our house toward the Tea House. I remarked, "That can't be good." I got up to go inside and met Mom at the bottom of the stairs. She had a very concerned look on her face. I'd seen that look only a couple of times in my lifetime, but I knew something was terribly wrong.

"We have a huge problem," she announced.

"What?" I felt my stomach grow tight.

"The whole back of the property is on fire. We have to get out now."

I couldn't believe it, so Beth and I jumped in our car and drove out of the courtyard around the back to the guesthouse. I'd never seen anything like it. Flames 200 feet tall were blowing around in 70mph wind. It was massive, barreling down from the Tea House—and we were directly in its path. Beth and I looked up in amazement at the sight, totally still and in shock. "It's going to take the house," was all I could say and think.

A few seconds passed, my mouth wide open, looking up at what used to be my playground in college. "Start praying," I told Beth. And with that, we both began to pray out loud. *Really* loud. We were literally "crying out to God." I whipped the car back into the courtyard, jumped out and ran inside. Mom and Harold stood in the entryway with Andrew and Aldona (our house managers) figuring out a plan.

"Get the van and bring it to the front," Harold told Andrew.

"Mom," I urged. "We have five minutes. What's the most important thing in the house?"

She was still looking at me in disbelief. "Nothing. We need to go."

I took charge and said, "Everybody, grab all the photos and photo albums. Go! Now!" We scattered like mice being chased by an alley cat. Beth was a great help because she had an advantage; she is 5'11" and could reach the photographs on the top shelves in the library. I grabbed an armful of photos off the walls and threw them in the back of my trunk. I came back in for another armful and noticed the portraits of Mom and Harold at the top of the stairs. Mom came by just then with her arms full of things.

"Mom, should I grab the portraits of you and Harold?" She said yes and dashed off outside.

I ran up the staircase skipping two stairs at a time in an effort to save time. A 30x40 portrait of Mom was on one side of the balcony, and another 30x40 portrait of Harold was on the other side. They were hanging rather high, so I stood on my toes and tried to unhook "Harold." I pushed with all my might and it finally came off the wall. I later realized both portraits were actually attached to the wall in case of an earthquake. No wonder I had such a struggle getting them off! I leaned "Harold" up against the wall and went for my mom next. I had recently had elbow surgery, but my adrenaline was running so high that I did not feel any pain until later. I quickly put "Mom" under my left arm and "Harold" under my right. As I took my first step down the stairs from the landing, the heavy portraits caught the first stair, and I was stuck!

I saw Beth running through the entrance hall with both arms full of photo albums and picture frames. She threw her load into the car and came back to help me. Meanwhile, I saw Andrew dart around the corner to the entry hall with an antique silver candelabra in each hand. He saw me on the stairs with Mom and Harold under my arms, obviously stuck.

"Amy, where do you want me to put these?"

I didn't hesitate and said, "In the pool," thinking that would be the safest place of all.

Andrew paused. "How about in the front yard in the grass?"

"They'll melt; throw 'em in the pool," I said as I handed Harold off to Beth and we ran to put both portraits in the van. We came back inside for what would be our last load before evacuating. I ran into one of the guestrooms and stood there trying to think clearly. I couldn't take all the photos—there were too many. So I took the older photos of my brother and me when we were young—the ones I knew we could not replace.

In about six or seven minutes, we all met at the front door after scrambling around and grabbing what we could take with us. Harold was characteristically calm and cool the entire time. Stoic as always, he never panicked and kept his wits about him. We took one last look around and Harold proposed, "Let's follow each other to the Biltmore Hotel (down in Santa Barbara and away from the fire). We'll have dinner there, and then we will figure out what to do."

Mom, Harold and Duke (their Springer spaniel) drove out of the courtyard toward the main entrance of the house. I decided to turn right to see exactly where the fire was at this point. Once again, Beth and I sat in the car mesmerized as we watched the flames and embers soaring across the night sky and over

> **"It says in the Bible to ask, so I'm asking God now to protect our home and hold back the flames."**

our heads. I had the window rolled down and, as if the flames could hear me, pleaded, "In the name of Jesus, please save the house if it's Your will. It says in the Bible to ask, so I'm asking God now to protect our home and hold back the flames." I think I even remember holding up my hands as if to hold off the flames. While I was praying out loud, so was Beth. I don't know what she was saying, but I know it was from her heart.

We finished praying, and I took one long last look at the house and yard, then we zoomed around to the side entrance on Cold Springs Road and left through the gate. It was dark as we pulled out, and we saw one lone fireman walking up the street. He was dressed head to toe in yellow protective gear. His fireman's helmet had a light on the front, and he was wearing goggles. He carried a flashlight and seemed to be looking for something. I jumped from the car, ran over to him, and asked what he was looking for. By now, the noise from the roaring fire and blustering winds were extremely loud, so I was yelling.

"I'm looking for people still in their homes," he yelled back. The fire was closer than before, right over us, and I could see it at the end of the street. "In no way do I want to put you in danger, but this is my house," I said and pointed over my shoulder. "What can I do to help you save it?"

"Get your gates open," he commanded me.

"Got it," I said and started back to the car. Then I turned around and put my hand on his shoulder. "I'm praying for you," I said and he thanked me.

I raced back to the car, threw it in reverse and drove backwards up the driveway at about 30mph in the dark. I had to get Andrew to open the back gate.

"Amy, you're going awfully fast," Beth said as she instinctively reached for the door handle.

"Don't worry, I've done this a thousand times," recalling all the years I'd lived there as a college student. I threw the car into park and ran up the back stairs to Andrew and Aldona's room. Andrew came running out to meet me. There was little time to spare.

"How can I get the back gate open and make it stay open for the fire trucks?"

"In the back of the gate, on the motor there is black

lever the size of your pinky finger. Pull that up, and it will release the gate."

While I was talking to Andrew, Beth got out of the car with her video camera, recording the embers raining down on the house and yard. In the video footage, you can hear her saying, "Oh no, this is bad…this is really bad. The embers are landing on the house…go away!" The fire was an orange glow in the sky, and all the embers floated around her.

I flew down the stairs from the back of the house so fast I think I only touched two or three of the steps. I passed my "videographer" friend and urged, "C'mon, Beth, let's go." I was fearless in that moment, determined to save our house. Beth told me later it reminded her of Todd Beamer, the 9/11 passenger whose inspiring last words were, "Let's Roll." I drove the car to the back gate where the fire was racing toward us. Although I knew I was running out of time, I was thinking to myself, "If I can get the back gate open, the fire trucks can come in and save the place." As we pulled up to the gate, it opened automatically. I crouched down and walked behind the gate into the bushes, lit only by the dull orange glow of the fire. The heat was stifling. I felt around in the dark and couldn't see anything like a lever. I looked again, frantically trying to put my hand on that lever. Suddenly my hand grazed something hard.

"I found it!" I yelled to Beth as I pulled and the gate began to open. The yellow-hued shadow of the encroaching fire fell across Beth's face. "We better get outta here, Amy."

I agreed. Embers were landing on the car and falling

on her hair. It was as if we were in a bad movie, with Beth and I in the leading roles. The smoke was thick all around us, and something inside me said, "Beth has a family…get her out of here." Just then, a big SUV pulled up behind us, and a man opened his door. "Amy," the man yelled. "Get down to the bottom gate! Your dad sent me up here to get you."

"I can't get out this way," I explained. The gate was only halfway open. The only way out was to go back down the driveway the way we came. After another ride backwards down the driveway, I turned around in the yard and headed to the winding hairpin-curved driveway at highway speed. We'd only been in California for about two hours, and Beth had had all the fun she could handle. As we hurled down the driveway, Beth said, "Does this normally happen?"

"No, not like this," I assured her and wiped soot off my forehead with the back of my hand.

We reached the front gate and, much to my surprise, Mom and Harold were standing next to the keypad pushing the code over and over. I hadn't thought about the power going out on the electric gate, leaving us stuck inside. I pulled up next to Mom.

"Where have you been?" she cried, thinking we'd be right behind her and Harold when they left.

"I was trying to get the gates open for the firemen," I explained, but it did not seem to erase any worry from her face. Beth got to experience "the look" that I have seen over the years anytime I do something dumb. Behind Mom were six cars in a semi-circle, with their headlights pointing at the gate and us. Little did I know that another actor and Montecito resident, Rob Lowe, had been trying to comfort Mom for the past 20 minutes while his house manager went looking for us. He was the one who found us and told us to get out of there. The six cars were all friends of my parents who live very close and knew the fire had started behind our house. They had risked their own lives to come up and make sure we were okay.

Mom instructed us, "Meet me at the Biltmore." I knew I was in big trouble. "Go straight there!" she added.

The traffic was horrible; there were sightseers and news reporters, fire trucks, police, and people walking around with horses and dogs that they had rescued from residents' property. When I made our way to the fire station (straight down from our house on Cold Springs Road), it was complete chaos. Cars were in a gridlock, people were honking, and policemen were yelling "Move it!" It was crazy. Several firemen were looking at a map, seemingly searching for alternate routes for the fire trucks. I looked at Beth and said, "Call and text all your prayer warrior friends. Ask them to pray for the safety of the firefighters, and ask that the Lord will save our house." We both started calling all the people we knew who would drop what they were doing and start praying for us.

> Although we were now stuck in traffic, the prayer chain spread like wildfire, no pun intended.

Although we were now stuck in traffic, the prayer chain spread like wildfire, no pun intended. Within 20-30 minutes after our calls and texts, I am sure about

150 people were praying for the firefighters, the house, and us. My friend, Dana Williams, texted me back Exodus 14:14, "The Lord will fight for you; you need only be still." Wow. What a great verse!

Since we weren't going anywhere anytime soon, I got out of the car and walked over to the firemen looking at the map. "Excuse me," I said and tapped one on the shoulder.

They looked up at me, worry creasing their foreheads. All around was chaos. I just said very calmly, "I want you to know, there is an army of people praying for you."

"Thank you," they said and got back to work.

At this point, I was the one now concerned about Mom and Harold's whereabouts. I had not seen them pass by, and I thought they were right behind us. "Stay here," I told Beth. "I'm going to see if I can find Mom and Harold." I walked back up Cold Springs Road and found them in a line of cars about eight-deep. When she saw me, Mom let me know that I needed to be "in my car and headed to the Biltmore." I didn't waste anymore time getting out of there!

We pulled up to the Biltmore behind Mom and Harold, and I made one more call to Sandy back in Texas. By now, it was late in the evening in Dallas. I knew it was awfully late to be calling, but I needed her "direct line" to God Himself. She gladly prayed with me over the phone. We said we loved each other, and I went straight back into the chaos that just hours before had been paradise.

The sky was radiant with color now, and smoke billowed all the way down to the ocean. We arrived at the Biltmore, but the fire was getting closer. Harold wisely said, "I don't want to eat here."

"How about the Wharf?" I suggested. 'We can get out on the water and see what's happening with the fire."

"Okay, follow me," he said, but we lost them almost immediately. Our cell phones were not working, so Beth and I made our way down to a beach road called Carrillo. We passed East Beach Grill and could see the Wharf a couple of miles away. At about 7:14, all the power went out in Santa Barbara. It was completely dark except for the glowing fire in the mountains. Even the traffic lights went out.

I thought it was scary up at the house near the fire, but this was ten times worse! With the incredibly strong wind, 15-foot long palm branches were falling in front of us onto the street, and we were all swerving around trying not to hit them. Cars were speeding through intersections without realizing it, then jamming on the brakes in order not to hit the cross-traffic. Between the howling wind and sirens, flying embers, screeching tires, exploding transformers, and maniac drivers, it was like being in the middle of Armageddon.

"Start praying we don't get hit from behind," I said to Beth, knowing all the ambulances and emergency personnel were on the mountain! That was the most defensive driving I'd ever done in my life. Thankfully, since I'd lived in Santa Barbara I knew where all the traffic lights were. I slowed to a stop, while the people behind and beside us would fly right through the middle, barely missing cross-traffic and the cars coming head on. It was intense, to say the least.

"Beth, just so you know, this is but a glimpse of what it

will be like in the End Times," I tried to joke. But I really wasn't kidding. As we made our way down Carrillo, the Wharf was in total darkness. I didn't know if Mom and Harold had already arrived before the power went out. I called Mom a dozen times, but no signals would go through. The Wharf closed just as we were pulling up, so I circled around and parked on Carrillo in front of another parked car. I did that so we would not get rear-ended by a panicked person who might be driving while texting! We sat there in silence—watching house after house, and tree after tree, go up in flames. The fire had now spread to at least five or six different locations because of the embers. The entire mountain before us was ablaze.

In a whisper I said, "I've never seen anything like this."

"Me neither," Beth responded.

Each time a 100-foot eucalyptus tree caught fire, it popped and exploded like a match soaked in gasoline. I knew there was not much hope for our home. Memories from the past 25 years flooded my mind. Some of the best times of my life were spent there. My cell phone suddenly interrupted my thoughts. *Holy cow! It worked!*

"Hello? Mom! Where are you?" I cried into the phone.

"Honey, we couldn't get on the Wharf, so we are headed for the highway. Get on the 101 and head to the airport." We decided to stay on the line to keep our connection going. I put my mom on speakerphone and laid the phone in my lap so I could drive.

"Everyone is panicked and trying to get out of town," I told her, steering around another palm tree as I made my way to the 101 freeway.

"I know, Honey, be careful," my mom cautioned.

Fire trucks continued to squeeze down the middle of the two-lane streets, rushing toward the mountains. We finally got to the freeway, cars zipping in and out of traffic. I looked in my rear view mirror. The sky was raging with flames and smoke. The nightmare was nowhere near over. Mom told us to meet at a restaurant called the Elephant Bar, a place we'd eaten at several years ago in the suburb of Goleta.

We pulled up right behind Mom and Harold, with Duke safely inside. We stood in the parking lot, still only 12 miles away from our home, and watched the flames that were now over the top of the mountain ridge. Only by the grace of God could our house survive. I knew God could do it, but was that His will? I hoped so.

> We sat there in silence—watching house after house, and tree after tree, go up in flames.

The people in Goleta were clueless about what was going on just 30 minutes away. I gave the lady our name to wait for a table and walked straight to the bar. Three televisions were showing local and national broadcasts of the fire. Homes were exploding into flames, and every eye in the bar was glued to the television reports.

Mom walked up next to me and swallowed hard, "Have you seen our house?"

"No, not yet," I said, my chest rattling with a deep cough. I had been too close to the fire too long; my eyes were burning and red, and I had a horrible, hurting cough from inhaling smoke.

"I can't watch," Mom said and turned away. "Let me

know if you see our house."

We were completely drained: mentally, physically, and emotionally. They sat us at a booth shortly after we got there, and a cute perky waitress bounced up to our table. "Hi. Welcome to the Elephant Bar," she said, oblivious. "What can I get you to drink?" Without making eye contact, Harold said, "You better bring us four martinis."

Beth whispered to me, "I've never had a martini before."

I whispered back, "Me neither. Tonight's the night."

It was hard to make conversation while silently wondering if our home (and all the memories inside) was burning at that very moment. After dinner, we headed to Bacara resort near Santa Barbara, but a safe distance away. We arrived with all the portraits, photo frames, and albums piled in the backseat and trunk, but no luggage. I just had a small bag with a few items I'd managed to grab. As we stood in the lobby waiting for our rooms, my cell phone rang again. It was 10:30 at night now, and I couldn't imagine who would be calling. I looked down at my phone and noticed it was an 805 area code. That was Santa Barbara.

"Hello?"

"Amy, it's Wayne," said the man who takes care of the property for Mom and Harold. I whispered to Mom, "It's Wayne." We both held our breath.

"I'm at your house—it didn't burn!"

My eyes filled with tears. I let out a loud cry and quickly covered my mouth. Mom and I were looking at each other, and she immediately put her hand over her mouth and began to cry. She thought the house had burned. But I was crying with joy, not grief.

"It's okay!" I said quickly and squeezed her hand. "The house made it!"

"I'm standing in the yard by the guesthouse," Wayne continued. "There is a fire truck in the yard, and they are putting out the flames now."

There was a huge collective sigh from all of us. Then Mom asked me with great anticipation, "Did my roses make it?"

"Wayne, did Mom's roses make it?" I asked, unsure what his answer would be considering all the embers and smoke.

"Yes, the roses are fine!" I nodded to Mom that they were okay. More tears. As I said before, Mom loves her rose garden.

Wayne assured us he would stay until he knew everything was okay, and we agreed to talk in the morning. In all, over 200 homes were destroyed and almost 2000 acres burned. But by His grace, God protected our home, even down to the last rose bush.

Morning could not come fast enough, and I was dying to get back to the house. We didn't know how our neighbors and friends were affected; communication was not easy, and by now it was getting very late. Beth and I collapsed in the beds in our rooms and watched the live news coverage of all the homes burning. It was heartbreaking and devastating to watch, but we couldn't take our eyes off the reports. We eventually turned the TV off, but I never fell asleep.

All night long, the helicopters flew just above us, filling their tanks with water and then heading over to the fire to douse the flames. My first text came at four o'clock in the morning. It was my brother checking to see if we were okay. It was two hours later where he lived, and he was watching the news. We talked briefly before text after text, and call after call, came rolling in from other friends checking on us.

The next morning, I walked next door to Mom and Harold's room and knocked. "Morning!" Harold was all smiles. I asked if they had slept at all, and Harold said he actually slept pretty well!

Mom came around the corner, "Morning, Honey." She was forcing her smile.

I told her Beth and I were headed to the house. "You want to come with us?" I ventured, knowing what her answer might be.

"Honey, no. We don't want to see it. I talked to Andrew, and he said the house is full of smoke and ashes. I don't think it would be a good idea for us to be up in all that. Especially Harold—he doesn't need to fill up his lungs with smoke. But will you get his medications and a couple of things from the house?"

I agreed to call them when I arrived. The TV reports were warning residents of roadblocks everywhere, so I knew it would take us a while to get there.

"Honey, please be careful," she said, a familiar refrain I'd heard a lot in my life. And I assured her I would. We hugged and kissed, I hugged Harold, and off I went.

As Beth and I came up Hot Springs Road, it initially looked okay, although it was eerily quiet. We reached

Sycamore Canyon and East Valley before we met our first roadblock. Policemen were on every corner with wooden roadblocks. Onlookers were creeping around, and the police were waving them off to one side or the other, not allowing them to continue up Sycamore Canyon, which is where we needed to go. I pulled up to the roadblock.

"Amy, what are you going to say?" Beth whispered.

"Just go with it," I said, not sure myself what I would come up with.

"Well, if anyone can get past the cops, you can," she said, smiling.

"Hi Officer," I said as I rolled down my window. "I live on Cold Springs Road, and I need to get some medication for my parents; it will just take a minute." He was not budging.

"Ma'am, we can't let anybody through. There are still fires burning and live electrical lines down."

> **"Honey, please be careful," she said, a familiar refrain I'd heard a lot in my life.**

I explained that Harold had to have his medication, and we needed clothes, too. "I'll be very careful," I added.

He looked at me intently then said, "Okay, but you can get a ticket if the Sergeant catches you. You go up at your own risk."

I thanked him and he moved the roadblock to one side.

"You can talk anyone into anything!" Beth said with a laugh.

We got to the house without being questioned, even though we passed a lot of police and fire trucks. The front gates were wide open as we drove up the driveway. The strong smell of smoke filled the air. As we got close to the house, we could see smoke rising from the scorched ground. Some trees were still smoldering, and some were still burning. There were firefighters all around using shovels to put out whatever was still aflame. We went into Mom and Harold's house first. It was dark, and all the shades were down. It was smoky and smelled like fire. I went to Harold's room to get his medication, and everything I touched was covered in a thick, gritty substance. The desktop, the legal pad, pens—everything had dark grime on it. When we got what we needed, we left and went to the guesthouse.

Helicopters and Coast Guard planes were flying overhead, but aside from the sound of their engines, it was very quiet. We went inside, and it smelled the same as my parents' home. We gathered our clothes and everything we had left behind. We walked around to the back of the guesthouse and noticed the fire had stopped only 30 feet away, although the rest of the back of the property had burned and was still smoldering. In fact, one of the neighbors was on our property putting out a tree with a garden hose. He was blessed, too—his home was still there. I thanked him, and we walked down again toward the main house.

As we walked along the creek bed that runs through the property, I was speechless. The trees, plants, bushes, and ground cover that had been there for so many years were gone. Completely gone. Everything was black. I could now see over to parts of our property I'd never seen before. Everything that remained was spitting out trails of smoke. As we got down toward the garage, I noticed God had spared that building as well. I looked over our wall to another neighbor's house. It was completely gone, except for the chimney, and flames still burned in the rubble.

The wind was blowing, and I was afraid those flames could flare up and come back to our side of the wall. Beth and I carefully walked through the smoldering remains of our yard, climbed the rock wall, grabbed that neighbor's garden house and began spraying the house (or what remained of it). The water pressure was so weak I had to push my fingers hard on the hose to spray it far enough to reach. In the meantime, Beth was taking pictures of everything, including me playing "firefighter." As I finished dousing the flames, a man pulled up beside the house and looked at the rubble. He got out of his car and said, "Oh my gosh...it's totally gone."

I introduced ourselves, fearing we may have pushed our limits since we were only supposed to be there for a few minutes getting Harold's medicine. But here we were, trespassing and playing firefighter. "Did you live here?" I asked sympathetically.

He shook his head. "No, I cleaned the pool here for the last 25 years. Mrs. Johnson lived here for 40 years." Forty years, I thought. Forty years of photographs, memories, everything she owned...gone. Destroyed. "Thank you, Lord" ran through my mind.

"Oh, I'm so sorry. Is she in town?"

"Yes, they barely got out in time," he replied, surveying the damage.

Beth and I walked with him around the remains up

to where the pool used to be. I have never seen such total devastation.

Conscious of our time, Beth and I then hiked back over the wall to our side and continued walking down the yard. We got to a place in the yard I always referred to as "Paradise." A waterfall and creek surrounded by big rocks runs through the lush green grass. There are huge ferns, tall trees, and beautifully colored flowers everywhere. Thankfully, it was still "Paradise"—it had not burned and was still green and lush! I stopped and looked around in awe. Between my feet and the green grass of Paradise stood a four-foot iron cross that Mom found at an antique shop. The fire had suddenly stopped about 30 feet before the cross. I couldn't believe my eyes. We were surrounded by black, burnt trees and burnt ground covering. Everything was black and charred from the fire, and then it just stopped.

Again, it was like a movie, but this was real. God stopped the flames from taking Paradise and the cross that stood in the middle of it. Then He stopped the fire from getting within 50 feet of the main house. People often said afterwards, "Thank goodness the wind changed direction, or it would have burned down your house." But I wanted to say, "Who do you think changed the direction of the wind? Hmmm…Who has that kind of authority?" In Matthew 8:24, the disciples asked after Jesus stilled a storm, "What kind of man is this? Even the winds and the waves obey him."

No one can tell me we are "lucky" that our house did not burn. The fire burned everything in its path on both sides of the house, but it did not get within 50 feet of the main house. Then it went on to the west and burned down 231 homes. We weren't "lucky." We were "blessed." God showed His grace and mercy on us, and this time the magnitude of His mercy was far beyond anything any of us had ever imagined. Let this story remind you today: "with God, all things are possible" (Matthew 19:26).

WHEN GOD SPEAKS

W HEN I MOVED BACK TO DALLAS IN 1991, MY friend, Dottie Poston, invited me to attend Bible Study Fellowship (BSF), a non-denominational Bible study for seekers, baby Christians, and longtime Christians who are familiar with God's Word. It is a great way to study Scripture and learn what the Bible says and also what it means. This study is not anyone's interpretation of the Bible; it's simply what the Bible clearly says. If you are looking to learn God's Word and what He has written to us through His followers, I highly recommend BSF or CBS (Community Bible Study). Both studies will meet you wherever you are in your spiritual walk.

At BSF, I met a girl in my small group named Michelle. During the course of the year, Michelle's forty-nine-year-old husband was diagnosed with multiple myeloma. Cancer. The doctors had prepared Michelle and Gary for the worst: he was going to die. However, I believed God wanted Gary to stay around a little longer.

Our small group prayed diligently for Gary. I would see Michelle from time to time as Gary was fighting the cancer and ask how he was doing. I prayed for them for months and months. After undergoing extensive treatment, and despite bad news from the doctors, he miraculously recovered. His cancer was gone, and we knew it was a total miracle. When he went into remission, we all rejoiced and thanked the Lord for what He had done. The doctors had no other explanation.

One night soon afterwards, I saw Gary and Michelle eating at a restaurant. I was so excited to meet the person for whom I had prayed so long. He looked great, and they were both smiling from ear to ear. I remember the joy I felt in my heart for them at the time.

I lost touch with Michelle after that. About a year went by, and one day I learned Gary was in the hospital again. He was still cancer-free, but his intense course of cancer treatment had taken a toll on his body, leaving his blood unable to coagulate. He contracted a simple urine infection in September and was now in the ICU. My heart broke, and I immediately began to pray—not just once a day, but all through the days and nights ahead. I remember driving home one day in a pouring rainstorm. A Christian song called "Why?" came on the radio by a group named 4Him. The lyrics touched my heart as they sang about the trials we sometimes go through. As the rain pounded on my windshield, I thought about how rain falls on each one of us at some point in life. As I listened to the words of the song, I began to cry. All I could think about was Michelle and Gary's struggle. Their faith in Christ sustained them, even in the worst of times. Their total trust in the Lord was very inspiring to the rest of us who watched and prayed from the sidelines.

I felt compelled to send the song I'd heard to Gary and Michelle, because the Lord impressed on me to do so. There was no doubt in my mind that it was Him, nudging me to go buy the CD and mail it to their home. I felt a bit hesitant, at first, because I didn't know how they would respond. I had not seen or spoken to Michelle in a year. Regardless, I turned the car around and drove to the nearest store to look for the song. I found it, tracked down Michelle's address, wrote a note with the CD, and told them to listen to that particular song.

> Their total trust in the Lord was very inspiring to the rest of us who watched and prayed from the sidelines.

I didn't hear back from them.

Weeks went by, and I heard the tragic news that Gary had passed away. I was afraid I had crossed the line by sending the song to them at the wrong time. But I had felt so strongly that I was supposed to do it. I didn't know why I never heard back, but I never stopped praying for them.

Several more months passed after Gary went home (his real home in heaven), and I still had not seen or spoken to Michelle. I noticed she did not come back to BSF, but I continued praying for her anyway. One day while sitting in a BSF lecture, I noticed out of the corner of my eye someone get up and leave the sanctuary. I looked over to see who it was...it was Michelle. I jumped up and went out into the lobby just as she reached the door. I called, "Michelle!" She stopped, and I told her how much I'd been praying for her.

"It's been very difficult," she said quietly. "Thank you for praying."

I wasn't sure if I should mention the CD, but then Michelle said, "Oh, I wanted to thank you for sending Gary that CD with the song. We played it every day in the ICU, and it helped ease our hearts and lift our burden. When he died, we played it again at his funeral."

My heart sank, my lips pursed, and tears began welling up in my eyes. As soon as she turned to leave, I ran outside to my car and cried out loud. I knew I'd felt led to send that gift that day. It was God nudging me to obey Him. That realization wasn't the only reason I was bawling, of course. I just felt so bad for Michelle. She was my age, and Gary was only fifty-two when he died, so young.

Remember the story when God had impressed my friend, Susan, to call me out of the blue during my temporary meltdown? Like me, she had to get out of her comfort zone to respond to God's leading. She'd called me just to say, "I want you to know I'm praying for you." In the same way, God used me to remind Gary and Michelle He was there. There is no way to know how many people were touched by that same song at Gary's funeral, and it showed their strength and faith in the Lord.

I later learned God had worked several miracles in Gary's life before he died. Toward the end of his life, he ended up in a "bubble room" at M.D. Anderson—a germ-free environment that protected him from infections because his immune system was shot.

The doctors injected him with his own stem cells to stimulate his immune system. For the 10 days he spent in the "bubble," no one could touch him or enter the airtight room. While he was there, a friend of his named Baron Cass called to wish him well. Gary was allowed a phone inside the room, which was his only way of communicating with others. When he answered, Baron tried cheering him up with a hearty, "How ya doin'?"

However, Gary did not hear what Baron was saying on the other line. Instead, Gary heard a calm voice say to him, "Be still, my son, I am here."

Confused, Gary moved the earpiece of the phone closer to his ear and said, "Hello?"

Baron repeated his hearty greeting, but once again Gary heard another voice speaking. The voice said, "Be still, my son, I am here." Gary was comforted by those words, convinced it was the Lord somehow speaking through Baron and into Gary's heart.

This story reminds me that God orchestrates everything in His timing, and He uses other people to bring us comfort and reassure us when we need it the most. We just have to have open eyes and hearts to see and sense His gentle nudges to get us to do something. And when we do, He works His plan through us. God uses people who are available to Him. If you are not aware of what is going on around you (and how God might be calling you), you will miss out on so many blessings. I can't explain the feeling when you are in God's will and He uses you for His purpose. But I will say there is peace and joy that comes from being blessed by God when you are in His will.

THE POWER OF HOPE

S ANDY, MY MENTOR, HAS TAUGHT A POPULAR BIBLE study class in Dallas for years. One of her classes was so good; I had to share it with you. She started her lesson by telling us a tragic story about a friend of hers whose daughter and granddaughter had car trouble while driving on a major highway. They pulled over to the shoulder and waited for help to arrive.

First, a man in an 18-wheeler stopped to lend a hand. He couldn't fix the problem, but he said he would go for help. He never returned. While the mother and nine-year-old daughter were waiting, another man showed up. To make a long story short, he raped both of them, shot them, and left them for dead on the side of the road.

Miraculously, they survived. However, the doctors said the little girl would be blind and unable to talk or walk. The bullet was in an inoperable place in her brain. Sandy went to visit the mom while she was in the hospital. Despite their tragedy, the mother's attitude toward God was inspiring. She said to Sandy, "I have chosen to trust Him with no explanation from Him— and no complaining from me. It's okay if I do not understand why, or if I do not hear from God."

Wow. That is a perfect example of faith and living the Christian life. God doesn't say life will be easy. He says, "Trust Me." That child is now thirty years old. She is married with kids of her own, and she can see, talk, and walk! Most of all, she has a strong, strong faith.

Having told this story, Sandy dove into Romans 8, a chapter about how Christians deal with life's challenges. A great, well-known verse for you to look up on your own is Romans 8:28—keep it in your heart and minds.

But here's another verse you may not know. Romans 8:18 (this is Paul talking) says, "I consider that our present sufferings are not worth comparing with the glory that will be revealed in us." Meaning, when we get to heaven (assuming you believe in Christ) all of the trials and difficult times will not seem so bad when we are filled with His glory, peace, love, comfort…all the things He promises us when we get there. We have *no idea* all the dangers God has kept away from us, but God also allows certain things, at certain times, to cross our path. We simply must desire to be in God's will either way.

God doesn't say life will be easy. He says, "Trust Me."

In fact, God desires for us to *want* to be in His will. Remember Job? If you are not familiar with his story, please read it in the Bible. No matter how difficult your situation may be, when you read about Job, you will feel much better and blessed! Job had everything, and God allowed Satan to take it away. By doing so, God was proving a point to Satan. He knew Job would be faithful and stand with God even during the worst of times. (You've got to read the story!)

Job reminds me of this family's incredible story of

faith. Somehow, their tragedy actually brought them closer to God in the end. When we step aside and let God be in control of our lives, He begins to transform us. Life is not a "do it yourself" project"! If you are going through a difficult trial, don't focus on the things you see or experience. Focus on what is going to last forever: eternity in heaven with God! Look beyond the hardships; God promises us His glory.

When God Intervenes in
DANGER

BEATING THE ODDS
WITH 132 STITCHES

I N 1983, I WAS A WILD AND REBELLIOUS EIGHTEEN-YEAR-
old. For graduation at the end of my senior year at
Highland Park High School, I got my dream car: a
Datsun 280ZX with t-tops and a boombox in the back. I
zipped around everywhere I went in that little sports car.
I thought I was so cool!

My friend, John McDaniel, held a graduation party one
night at a nice private restaurant called The Lancers Club
in downtown Dallas. His date was my best friend, Cynthia
Love. John had just received the keys to his graduation
gift as well—a beautiful Riviera. We decided to follow
each other to the party in our brand new cars. It just so
happened that my mom was out of town that weekend,
visiting friends with Harold. When I was getting ready
for the big party, I decided to take advantage of the fact
that my mom was gone. Her black-and-white checked fur
vest looked so vulnerable, hanging there all alone in her
closet. *She will never know I wore it,* I thought to myself
as I took it off the hanger. And boy, did it look good over
my white lace shirt!

My date was Dan and the four of us headed out for
the party about seven that night. I was following John and
Cynthia as we zoomed down Turtle Creek Boulevard, a
beautiful winding street with huge trees lining the way. As

we approached a condo building called the Warrington, I noticed the sprinklers were on, leaving a trail of water streaming across the street. One second later, John and Cynthia hydroplaned and hit a large tree in the median. Both of them simultaneously flew out through the windows onto the median. Their bodies looked like rag dolls, and I couldn't believe my eyes.

Immediately, my car also began swerving from side to side. "Slow down!" Dan yelled. I was turning the wheel as fast as I could, steering back and forth trying to pull us out of a tailspin. My headlights were shining on John's car, which now rested against the tree. Everything was happening in the blink of an eye; I couldn't stop us, even though I tried my best. Spinning out of control, we were now headed straight for John's car at a speed that made NASCAR look slow. Suddenly all went black. Silence.

I landed on Dan's seat—my head on his headrest and my body stretched across the car. Cynthia and John were still sprawled in the median; my car and John's were now one. Fortunately, Cynthia had managed to put her arm in front of her face before she went through the window of John's car, but she was moaning and bleeding, unable to get up. John finally stood to his feet and walked across the street to the Warrington. He dialed the number of The Lancers Club (this was before cell phones) to reach his dad, a doctor, who was waiting there for us along with eight of our closest friends. One of the waiters answered the phone and John asked for his dad. The waiter could tell something was wrong and went to find John's dad.

"Dr. McDaniel, you have a call," the waiter said urgently.

"I'm not taking any calls right now," his dad said,

thinking it may have been work.

"Dr. McDaniel," the waiter said firmly, "it's your son. He says it is an emergency." With that, John's dad jumped to his feet and went to the phone. When he returned to the table, he told our friends to start dinner without him because he and his wife had to leave. Of course, our friends were freaking out because we never showed, and they knew John had called about an emergency.

Back at the accident, Dan got out of the car and checked on us. He was always great at handling tragic situations. Cynthia was moving slowly, but she was alive. He opened my car door to see about me. I was unconscious, but he thought I was dead. He tore off the rearview mirror of my car and held it up to my mouth to see if I was breathing, and luckily I was. He put his hands around my head to try and straighten it out. When he touched my head, both of his hands sank inside the back of my skull.

My head had hit the glass t-top on the roof of the car, splitting my scalp from top to bottom. The split was about seven inches long and ended right at my neck. Thinking quickly, Dan took off his shirt and wrapped it around my head to try and stop the profuse bleeding. My lifeless body now lay in my demolished dream car, my mom's vest covered in blood and laced with tiny shards of glass.

Soon the ambulance arrived, and the EMT began working on me. While all of this was happening, Cynthia's mom and dad "just happened" to drive down the same street on their way to dinner and saw the wreck. Neither of them recognized the cars, which looked like a twisted mess of metal. They drove by, but two blocks later, Karen was unable to get that image out of her mind.

She said, "Honey, which way do you think the kids went to the Lancers Club?"

Her husband, Ross, looked at her and said, "Do you want to go back and check?" Worried, they turned around and headed back to the wreck to see if those were our cars.

They pulled up on the opposite side of the street, and Ross got out of the car. Just as he approached the ambulance, he recognized his daughter, Cynthia. He went back to the car, leaned in and softly said to Karen, "It's our baby."

Karen ran to the ambulance just as they were securing Cynthia's gurney beside mine and began talking to us. I heard a familiar voice talking, but I could not figure it out. It was a voice I knew…soft, sweet, and comforting. My eyes were still closed, but I could hear everything going on around me. I thought I had bitten off my tongue, now a large, soft lump in my mouth. In a daze, I reached my hand to my mouth and handed the lump to the familiar voice behind me. (Fortunately, I later learned it was only my gum!) This gentle voice continued to comfort me with positive words. "Call my mom," I said to her.

Soon I felt someone else squeezing my hand. "Amy, Amy…talk to me," this other voice said. "You're going to be okay. Open your eyes and look at me. Amy, Amy, wake up!" This time the voice was Cynthia's, who was next to me on a gurney, holding my hand. I remember looking up into the EMT's eyes. He was looking into mine with a flashlight.

"What's your name?" he asked, trying to assess how badly I was hurt.

"Is my car okay?" was all I could think to say.

He smiled. "Well, it's pretty banged up," I heard him say before I slipped into an unconscious fog again. Blackness. Silence.

I woke up sometime later and thought, "What is tugging on my head?" More tugging. "Ouch, my head hurts! Who is pulling on my head?" I was no longer in the ambulance, but I couldn't speak.

"I'm glad we got to her when we did," a strange voice said. "She's lost a lot of blood. About two or three pints, I'd say."

My eyes were still closed. I was now stretched out on a cold, hard surface, while the doctors were stitching up my wound and pulling my scalp back together. Then once again, everything went to black.

It was a voice I knew...soft, sweet, and comforting.

I don't know who called my dad, probably the Loves. Cynthia and I had been best friends since first grade, and Karen was like my second mom. My parents were divorced, and for the first time ever, my mom "just happened" to give my dad the phone number where she and Harold were staying that weekend. From the hospital, my dad called Mom at her friends' house to let her know what happened to me.

"Hello?" my parents' friends answered.

"Is Annette there?" my dad asked. "This is Larry Fleck." They put him on hold while they went to find my mom.

"Annette," they said to Mom while she sat at the dinner table with several others, "Larry Fleck is on the phone for you." Her heartbeat tripled, and the blood drained from her face. She knew something was really wrong for my dad to be calling.

"Annette," he began, "it's Amy. She's been in a car wreck." Dad began to cry on the phone, and Mom put her head between her legs so she wouldn't faint. The rest of the dinner party fell silent.

"Is she alive?" Mom asked, hopeful.

"She is in surgery," my dad explained.

"Is she going to make it?"

At that, Dad burst into tears. "They didn't say...she hit her head."

Mom hung up the phone and summoned all her "Mommy strength" to go back to the table and inform her friends what had happened. She and Harold went into the other room where Mom began praying. She asked Harold when they could fly out, thinking he'd be able to take them right away since he had flown his plane there.

"Darling," he said and took her hands, "we can't take off tonight. The airstrip is closed at night. We will have to wait until the morning." Mom was devastated. I was in surgery, she was not sure if I was going to make it, and she couldn't get home until the next day.

Back at the hospital, two nurses approached my dad. "Mr. Fleck, would you like to see your daughter?" They brought Dad into the ER room where they had just taken x-rays of my skull. I heard an unfamiliar voice of a hospital worker say, "Amy, your father's here." It was all I could do to open my eyes. Dad stood over me, tears falling from his eyelashes onto my shoulders.

"Hi Dad," I barely muttered.

"Baby, you're going to be okay. I love you," he said. Just then, I caught a glimpse of my face in the reflection of the x-ray machine above my head. My face was covered in blood, and there was a small puncture under my nose spewing blood everywhere. They whisked Dad out of the room and worked to stop the bleeding, soaking several gauze pads. Blackness. Silence. Unconscious again.

The next thing I knew, people were trying to get me to sit up. "Sit up?" I thought. "I don't know where I am, and my head is killing me for some reason."

It took two or three nurses to get me to sit up and maneuver myself into a wheelchair. They wheeled me to a sink and told me they needed to rinse my hair.

"Where was I, the beauty parlor?"

Before I knew it, they were holding my limp body over an oversized sink. When they bent me over, the pressure inside my skull was so strong and painful I thought my head was going to pop off into the sink! (Actually, I was hoping it *would* pop off—maybe that would relieve the horrible pain I was feeling.) I managed to open my eyes as the warm water washed over my head, but then I saw the sink was full of blood.

While my head was upside down in the sink, I also caught a glimpse of Mom's blood-soaked fur vest. I wasn't sure what had happened, but a wave of nausea came over me, and I began to vomit profusely.

I just *thought* my head hurt before—now it was really hurting! I passed out in the arms of the nurses. Dan was in the waiting room of the hospital. He had his jacket on, no shirt, and was clinging to the one shoe I had on when I arrived at the hospital. Eventually, they released me from the ER, and Dan and Dad brought me home. However, I do not remember anything past when the vomiting started.

I woke up early the next morning, and I was in my room. It was unusually bright; all the shades were open. I was almost sitting up in the bed, with several pillows stacked behind me. Dan and Dad were sitting in chairs on either side of the bed, keeping watch. Dan was still in his suit from the night before, and Dad was smiling at me from his side of the bed. "Hi Baby, how are you feeling?" he asked.

Why are they in my bedroom? I thought. (Boys were not allowed in my room!) I was trying to figure out what was going on. *Why is Dan in a suit with no shirt on? And why is it so bright in my room?* (The boys didn't lower the shades when they brought me home.) *Why does my head hurt? Why is everyone staring at me?*

While I was still trying to solve this mystery, Mom entered the room. I still remember the look on her face, reminiscent of the time she saw the fire coming towards our house. Deeply concerned, her eyes never left mine. She went straight to my side and gently touched my face with her hand. My head was wrapped in a white turban, and I had over 132 stitches. (Thank the Lord they were not in my face.) I suffered memory loss and a concussion. The memory loss was so frustrating. I couldn't remember any of the things I knew that I knew. School was almost out, and all my teachers exempted me from my final exams except for one. If I passed her final, I do not know, but I passed her class and that's all that mattered.

For months, the memory loss and pain in my head lingered. Several times a year, I still have a tingling feeling like mice running over my scar. The doctor told me that several nerve endings were severed in the crash. Whenever I feel that sensation, it's just the cut nerves sending signals searching for their other half. Every time I experience that odd feeling, it reminds me how God protected me and saved me for a reason. He could have easily brought me home that night, but His plans were to let me live and pass these stories onto you. God is real, and He protects His children.

By the way, it turns out Mom could not have cared less about her fur vest. It spent five months at the cleaners, and she gave it to me for Christmas that year. I still have it in my closet, and every time I see it, I say, "Thank You, Lord."

WOMEN IN THE WINE COUNTRY

IT WAS THE ULTIMATE GIRLFRIENDS ROAD TRIP. MY FRIEND, Paige, had invited me on a trip to Paris, San Tropez, and Monte Carlo in the summer of 1998 with two of her friends from college, Jackie and Chantell. I barely knew her college friends, but Paige and I had traveled together quite a bit. Plus, we went to the same church and Bible studies.

Paige is one of my "funnest" friends, if you know what I mean. She is always up for an exciting adventure. If you're having a birthday party, she's the kind of friend you want on your invitation list because she will elevate the "fun factor" ten times. Paige is a beautiful girl, inside and out, and she loves to dress up in designer clothes with matching shoes and purses. In fact, all those girls could have daylong dueling fashion shows with their beautiful boutique designer clothes.

Me? Not so much. I love cute clothes and shoes like any other girl, don't get me wrong. But Paige and I differ greatly in the clothing department. I'm much more comfortable being casual and comfortable. We're also different because I'm quick to respond in a crisis, and she is very laid back and unaffected by urgent matters. I like to be on time; she runs an hour late. That is why she earned the nickname, "Chopper." I'm constantly saying, "Chop, chop! Hurry up," clapping my hands quickly in rounds of two. Actually, we refer to each other as "Chopper" because she says I "chop" her to get going! They say opposites attract, and we couldn't be more different. But we both love to travel and have fun. More importantly, we both love the Lord. When the four of us set out for France, I had no idea what I was in for.

We arrived in Paris and spent three nights there. Then we rented a van for me to drive us out to the wine country. When we went into the rental company office to retrieve our van, we received a surprise. Did you know Paris does not have vans or SUVs? We didn't.

"What, no SUVs? What kind of place is this?" we wondered. We were from Texas—the birthplace of four-wheel drive—and we just assumed every country had them. Instead, we got the keys to a very small, four-door hatchback Volvo. With no bellhop and three fashion queens in tow, we began trying to stuff 18 suitcases into a sardine can. It took all four of us pushing just to shut the hatchback. The girls' feet were slipping in the street because their high heels had no traction. The young man who rented us the car watched from inside, not about to offer to help the four Americans. After we heard the "click" of the now filled-to-capacity hatchback, we squeezed into our seats.

I was familiarizing myself with the car, while Paige manned the CD player and looked over the directions. We headed out from the rental car parking lot straight into a six-street roundabout. We circled very slowly, looking for the right French name on the street signs. We made a complete circle and were back in front of the rental office. Slowly, we made another round, but we could not see which way to go!

Once again, we were back at the rental office. "Budget boy," as we'd begun calling him, was still watching. We headed out for a third time into the roundabout, this time deciding to chance it and take one of the streets. I'm sure Budget boy was glad to see us go.

> **With no bellhop and three fashion queens in tow, we began trying to stuff 18 suitcases into a sardine can.**

We came out onto the main street in Paris, the Avenue des Champs-Élysées, right by the Arc de Triumph. It was a racecar driver's dream: five unmarked lanes of traffic and no speed limit! I'm not so sure my passengers were as excited as I was though. All I heard was, "Watch out...Slow down!...Turn here...Wait...Go!...Do you know where you're going?"

Of course I did not know where I was going; I was in Paris, France, driving a four-door hatchback and couldn't see out of the back window!

We flew through Paris and finally found our way to the right autobahn. Paige was the navigator and our personal GPS. After driving for 30 minutes or so, we came to what seemed to be some kind of tollbooth with a gate. The bar lifted up when we pulled up, but there was no one at the booth, so I drove through. We were rocking out to music, enjoying the beautiful green countryside and trees. About 45 minutes later, we came to another tollbooth, except this time there was a lady inside the booth. We pulled up and she said, "Bonjour."

"Bonjour," I said back with a smile.

"Si vous play…" she began speaking in French.

A blank look came over my face. "What?"

"Si vous play…"

"How…much…do…we…owe?" I interrupted in English, trying to let her know we did not speak French.

Her head turned like a dog that had heard a high-pitched scream. We uselessly exchanged English and French for several minutes before she called the police. Next thing we knew, a bar came down in front of the car and one in the back, trapping us in the tollbooth.

In a moment, five policemen dressed in all-white uniforms with tall white hats and white boots walked over to our hatchback. It must have been a slow day for them. They bent over and inquisitively looked into our car. I quietly said to the girls in the backseat, "Look up 'How much?' in the dictionary." We had an English/French dictionary of short phrases. By now, the policemen had taken off their hats and were scratching their heads as they peered in the open windows. The four of us were scrambling for money and words.

Chantell began to sound out the words in French. She said words that sounded French enough, but I had no clue if they were the right ones.

The policemen looked at each other, then at the French lady in the booth. They seemed confused as they began to chatter back and forth in French. Jackie whispered something to me and I started laughing.

"What are you guys saying?" Chantell asked innocently.

The policemen were not laughing. I braced myself for the worst.

Jackie spoke up between laughs, "Chantell, you just said, 'How bizarre?' not "How much?'"

At this point, I'm thinking the fashion queens and I were going to end up in a French prison. After 20 minutes of trying to decipher what we were trying to say, the policemen finally let us go. (That was also after we gave them five dollars.) Later, we discovered that we should have grabbed a ticket in the first tollbooth upon entering. The second tollbooth collects money for the amount of time you spent on the autobahn. I can tell you, at the speed I was going, we probably owed only a few pennies at the most. I love to drive fast, and with not much of a speed limit, "Amy-O-Andretti" was pushing the limits!

Nevertheless, we eventually made it to the wine country in Beaune, France. Beautiful fields with rows of grapes filled the rolling hills, and Mom and Pop stores were scattered along the roads. While we were touring one day, we ended up on a gravel road so narrow I was sure it was a one-way road. The music was still on, and Paige was navigating us to some wineries with cute little outdoor lunch cafés. As I turned left around a blind corner on the one-lane road, to my shock and horror I saw another car coming at me. I swerved to the right to try to avoid a collision but quickly realized the road dropped off there. So, I whipped the wheel back to the left, thinking I'd rather the car hit me than us go over the cliff. As I swerved back to the left, the other car rammed our little hatchback and pushed us to a stop only six inches away from the cliff.

I heard the girls screaming, glass breaking, and that horrible sound of two cars colliding. When we came to a stop, I said, "Is everybody okay?" Everyone was still screaming and discombobulated.

"Is everyone okay?" I repeated, this time a notch louder. They were all fine.

"Which window broke?" I asked next, remembering the sound of shattered glass.

"It was the wine glasses on the floor from yesterday's winery," Jackie said. Whew. Jackie said that her life had just flashed before her eyes, and I knew what she meant. My heart was beating out of my chest. My entire body was shaking, and I was breathing double time. I got out of the car, my knees knocking, and walked to the edge of the gravel road. Our tires were six inches from going straight over the side of a six-foot drop. Had we gone over the edge in the luggage-packed hatchback, I feel certain it would have caused major injuries or even death. The young French couple that hit us got out of their car, and we greeted each other though we were all still frightened.

His car had a rather large dent in the front left bumper where he'd hit our car. My mind was racing. *Do we have insurance? Yikes! Do we call the police? (I don't speak French. They don't speak English.) No cell phones, and we are in the middle of nowhere—double yikes!* As I looked over the hatchback, I couldn't find a dent anywhere. I know he hit us because I heard it and felt it as his car pushed us to the edge. I examined our vehicle closely at every angle. Nothing. I was confused.

I bent down to see the back left tire and noticed a thumbnail-size gash in the hubcap. "Surely, that's not all that happened," I thought in disbelief. The couple and I exchanged glances and shrugged our shoulders as if to say, "Oh, well." They got back in their car and drove off very slowly. I walked up to the window of our car and said, "If you don't believe in God, come look at this." The girls worked their way out of the car and walked to the front to see where we almost slid off.

"This is a flat out miracle that we didn't go over the edge," I concluded. Everyone agreed. We then packed ourselves back inside the undamaged car, but I was still a nervous wreck. To this day, we realize God had His hand on us. There is no doubt that the Lord intervened for us once again that day and brought us safely back home.

Nothing Good Happens after Midnight

WHEN I WAS A YOUNG GIRL IN HIGH SCHOOL AND college, my mom always said, "Nothing good happens after midnight." I'd usually roll my eyes and say, "Oh, Mom. When the clock strikes 12:00, does the boogie man come out?" A couple of times she responded matter-of-factly that yes, he does. And one evening on that same girls trip overseas, I found out she was right.

I always had a 12:00 curfew, even after college. However, when I was in Paris with my friends Paige, Jackie, and Chantell, we went to dinner and then to a disco for some late night dancing. Paige loves to dance off the calories after dinner, so it's pretty much a given that when you go out to dinner with Paige, you'd better put on your dancing shoes. If you have never been to Europe, let me give you a "heads up." They don't eat dinner until 10:30-11:00 at night. The discos don't really get going until two in the morning! Needless to say, it was already late when we hit the discotheque.

Jackie and Chantell were smart; they went home after about an hour. Paige and I stayed way too long. It was definitely "after midnight" then. We were young and single, and we met some cute Middle Eastern guys while we were there and talked with them for a short while. When we finally decided to go home, Paige and I walked out to get a cab. The streets and sidewalks were full of people, and the outdoor cafés were full—even at four in the morning.

Suddenly, a white BMW zoomed up right beside us. One guy was driving, and one was in the backseat. Before I knew what was happening, two more boys flanked Paige and me. They were the boys we met at the disco. My radar went up and I thought to myself, "Something bad is about to happen." Seconds later, the boy next to Paige picked her up from behind and began stuffing her in the back window of his car. The boy inside the car was trying to grab her feet, and she was screaming, "Amy, help! Amy, don't let them take me!"

I was also screaming, "Let her go! Let her go!" and began beating the boy on his chest as hard as I could with my fist. Paige instinctively propped her feet on top of the car, preventing him from shoving her inside. Her back was against the boy's front as he held down her arms and tried to push her in the window. The fourth boy was trying to get me off the boy holding Paige. I was screaming so loudly, but nobody would help us. This struggle went on for what seemed like 20 minutes (but was probably less than 90 seconds).

Everything happened so quickly. All I knew to do was to scream and hit. Then, for

> "Oh, Mom. When the clock strikes 12:00, does the boogie man come out?"

unknown reasons, the boy suddenly put Paige down. We ran toward a silver Mercedes cab about 40 feet in front of the boys' car. I remember turning around to see if they were chasing us. They were running full speed toward us as we flung open the door to the cab and jumped into the backseat. We screamed to the driver, "Go, go, go!" and looked out the back window—the boys were still running after us!

When they realized they couldn't catch us on foot, they ran back to the car and resumed the chase. Paige and I crouched down in the back of the cab holding each other, completely hysterical. The cab driver drove like a typical cab driver would: fast and crazy—taking the corners on two wheels. Even so, the boys caught up to us in their car and were right on our tail. The cabbie took us down alleyways, around corners, everything he could do to lose these guys. He must have been an angel. Most cabbies would have said, "Get out, I don't need this!" However, he took care of us, knowing he too could have been in danger. I'm just thankful he was not involved with the boys somehow. He could have easily let us out in the alley for the boys to have an easy pick up.

After a hair-raising 20-minute car chase, we lost them. We drove around for quite a while longer to make sure they were gone before going back to our hotel.

If God had not intervened, I shutter to think about what might have happened. *What if they had managed to get Paige in the car? Was I next? Would they have taken her and left me? Would I have ever seen her again? What were they going to do with her?* After I saw the movie, *Taken* (about a girl who finds herself in a similar kidnapping situation) I realized just how awful it could have been. I've run from trouble several times, but I know for a fact that God intervened. He was with us, protected us, and saved us from horrific things that could have happened—things I try not to think about.

There is no doubt in my mind that God had His hand and His angels around us. Psalm 31:14–15 says, "But I trust in you, O Lord; I say, 'You are my God.' My times are in your hands; deliver me from my enemies and from those who pursue me." And Psalm 40:13, 17 says, "O Lord, come quickly to help me. You are my help and my deliverer; O my God, do not delay."

God takes care of us even when we don't realize it until later. As I look back over my life, I see how God intervened so many times. In some of the situations where God rescued me, I realized it immediately and thanked Him right then. At other times, I didn't realize the danger and couldn't see how God rescued me, until years later. Some people claim to have nine lives. I think I have had about 50. God has been so gracious with me over the years and has covered me with His protection. And for that, I am truly grateful.

"For he will command his angels concerning you to guard you in all your ways," Psalm 91:11.

MARK ONE OFF
THE BUCKET LIST

IT'S CRAZY. I DON'T KNOW WHY, BUT ALL MY LIFE I HAVE loved mini-bikes, mopeds, and motorcycles when I got older. I rode my first mini-bike (a smaller version of a motorcycle) at the age of eight years old. Mom was a decorator, and she was decorating a lake house one summer in a new development in Tyler called Holly Lake Ranch. We stayed with some friends who happened to have mini-bikes, and I was enamored with them. My sweet dad spent long, hot, dusty days watching me as I rode around and around the driveway. I still have the T-shirt Dad made me for Christmas one year with a picture of me and the mini-bike printed on the shirt! To this day, it's one of my favorite photographs!

My love for mini-bikes soon evolved into mopeds (a motorized bike). When I was a teenager, Harold gave me a bright orange Honda Express in the eighth grade. He and mom were just dating then, but he already had my vote! As I grew older, I continued to feel the need for speed, but this time I wanted something faster— something I could jump some bumps with. As God would have it, Harold enjoyed riding motorcycles, too. He just happened to have a couple of them at his place in Ozark, Arkansas. I'll never forget my first trip with Mom and Harold to Ozark. We pulled up to the "double wide" trailer, and the front yard was full of motorcycles and off-terrain vehicles. As a kid, I wasn't that impressed with the fact Harold could fly his own plane, but he had motorcycles!

My favorite was the Suzuki 125. It didn't take me long to learn how to work the clutch and gearshift. Then I was off riding all over the property for the rest of the day. I remember telling my mom, "Mom, this is so cool! This is the fastest I've ever been on a motorcycle." I went as fast as the 125 could go and hung on, the wind flapping my cheeks. It wasn't too long before Harold showed me my first "jump." We would go really fast up a super steep hill to a point where it leveled off and catch "big air!" Mom would stand at the top and watch so we wouldn't collide as we went up and down. This is when my love for motorcycles really began.

My mom has been awesome through all of my adventuresome endeavors. I can't begin to imagine what

I put her through as the parent of a wild, rebellious, try-anything-once little girl. I know one thing though; she spent many days and hours on her knees, asking God to please protect me. Mom's prayers worked. God has protected me through all my crazy adventures, including: scuba diving to a wrecked sunken ship, motorcycling, skiing on "expert only" slopes, bungee jumping, sky diving, paragliding, and the list goes on. Thank You, Lord, and thank you, Mom!

Since I was thirteen years old, we started going as a family to Aspen, Colorado. I loved watching people race up Aspen Mountain on their colorful dirt bikes, dressed in motorcycle gear from head to toe: helmets, chest protectors (that matched their helmets), elbow pads (that matched their chest protectors and helmets), knee and skin guards (that matched their elbow pads, chest protectors, and helmets).

I rode my first mini-bike at the age of eight years old.

To top it off, they wore cool-looking motorcycle boots (the six-buckle ones that come up to your knees), which matched everything, too. As each summer went by, I watched the riders from my balcony going up and down the mountain and dreamed of the day I would do it, too. It seemed impossible, namely because I didn't have a dirt bike in Aspen. And I didn't know anyone who had one. So, it wasn't until just a few years ago that my childhood dream came true.

∞

In July of 2007, I heard about a place called Mountain Adventures that rented four-wheelers and motorcycles. I was staying in Aspen for about a month and immediately called to see what was available.

"Mountain Adventures, this is William," the clerk answered on the first ring.

"Hi!" I said, breathless with excitement. "I was wondering if you rent motorcycles."

"Yes, we do." Big smile. "We have a Honda XR 250 and four-wheelers."

Music to my ears. "Great! I'd like to rent the Honda to go up Aspen Mountain."

I arranged for William to bring the Honda to the home where I was staying. When he arrived, he stepped out of his white pick-up truck wearing jeans and boots. He had sandy blonde hair that resembled John Denver's back in the eighties. I saw he had a pack of Camel cigarettes in his pocket, and he was nearly six feet tall. He smiled sweetly, extended his hand and said, "Hi, I'm William. But you can call me Bill if you want. You must be Amy." He unloaded the red and white Honda 250 and his huge, green four-wheeler. He'd already suggested he go with me, which I was happy for him to do since I wanted to go with someone with experience.

Telling Mom about my adventure was out of the question. *No need to worry her*, I told myself. I didn't have all the matching gear—just a helmet, some gloves I'd bought at the bicycle shop in town, hiking boots, jeans, and a blue jean jacket. I was not quite prepared for the day ahead, but off we went, riding through town up to the base of Aspen Mountain.

My heart was beating extra beats as I looked at the side of the mountain: steep dirt and rocky roads all the way up. I played John Denver's "Rocky Mountain High" on my mobile phone, in honor of my Rocky Mountain adventure! I have to admit I was slightly nervous—given the fear of the unknown. However, once I shot up the first part of the road, my adrenaline was boiling with excitement. I had flashbacks of riding in Ozark on the dirt bike.

I can do this, I thought as I steadily navigated the exceptionally rocky terrain. *Ozark was more dangerous than this,* I assured myself. Every once in a while, I'd looked down the mountain at the town and see the house where our family once owned a home. It was easy to spot because it was a block from "Gazebo" park. Thirty years of great memories from Aspen ran through my mind as John Denver sang in my ears.

We got to the top in just 25 minutes, instead of the hour or two I thought it would take. I pulled over at the skiing gondola, William right behind me. I took off my helmet and shouted, "That was awesome! I loved it!"

"You wanna keep going?" William said. "There's more. We can ride clean to Crested Butte."

"Awesome!" I replied. "Let's go!" I knew Taylor Pass is a beautiful place, and William said it would take us a couple hours to get there.

"Let's go there and see how that goes," he said. I had a sip of water, put my helmet back on, and sped away.

After 30 years of coming to Aspen, I never knew what was beyond the gondola. "Wow," was the first thing that came to my mind. When I lived in Aspen, I'd skied behind the gondola on big snow days on a run we called "Pandora's Box." If you hike beyond the gondola on the left, you can cross under a rope with a sign that reads, "Out of bounds. Ski at your own risk." Naturally, my friends and I would always ski there on powder days. Some days, the snow would come up to our chests—now that was awesome!

On the motorcycle, I went far past Pandora's Box, headed way up the mountain. We soon arrived at a beautiful field covered in wildflowers. I slowed down to look around and take it all in; William pulled up and said, "You want to take a picture?" I'm a professional photographer...of course I wanted a picture!

He took a couple of pictures of me with the field in the background: wildflowers, Christmas trees, and snow-capped mountains. I couldn't think of a word to accurately describe the beauty God had made and allowed me to enjoy. Several times while I was riding I prayed, "Lord, thank You for this incredible place of beauty. Thank You for allowing me the opportunity to be here and experience all You created for me!" I remember speeding along and yelling out in praise, "Woo-hoo!" many times. I couldn't help it! I was experiencing my dream after 30 years!

We made it to the top of one of the peaks and got off our vehicles to stretch our legs. Within a few minutes, it began to sprinkle, then rain. I had no rain gear. It grew dark, the wind picked up, and it began lightning all around us. William showed no urgency or fear, but I wasn't too sure about being on a mountain peak standing next to two metal objects during a lightning storm. "Should we take cover?" I asked.

"Yeah," he said, looking around for a good place. "Let's ride down to that clump of trees."

It was now pouring rain, and we quickly rode to a nearby thick forest for shelter. The drops felt like toothpicks pricking my face. We rode into the middle of some tall trees and got off the vehicles. The trees helped some to protect us, but the thunder and lightning were getting louder and closer. While we waited for the storm to pass, we talked about our families and our lives. I found out he was a bull rider and a rodeo clown! He also told me he almost lost his family due to a drinking problem. He had been sober 12 years, and I congratulated him on making that decision and sticking to it. He had a genuine, sweet heart and also appreciated living in one of the most beautiful places in the country. When the storm passed, we continued our journey to Taylor Pass.

> Thirty years of great memories from Aspen ran through my mind as John Denver sang in my ears.

An hour or so into the ride, we rounded a corner and I noticed the road suddenly went straight up through rocks, with several sharp turns. The rocks were about the size of softballs and footballs and they littered the trail. I never thought twice about the severity of the terrain; I just kept going right on up. About a third of the way, my front tire caught a rock that caused my motorcycle to flip sideways. When I stopped, my front tire was inches from going off the side of the trail. I looked down about 20 feet below and thought, "Holy smokes, that would have hurt if I'd gone over."

I looked down at William, who was behind me. "You

all right?" he called.

"Yeah, I'm good," I said, muscling my handlebars to start backing up.

"You need some help?" he tried again.

"No, I got it." I was backing up the bike as best I could on the rocks.

He offered again to take over, and I declined. So, he just sat and waited. After I backed up pretty far, I turned the wheel and hit the gas. I got about 15 feet higher and the same thing happened. This time, it was so steep my right foot wouldn't touch the ground. I looked down at William again.

"You want me to take it from here?" he asked, a worried expression on his face.

"No, no. I can do it," I said, grimacing and straining to reach my toe on a rock to gain some balance.

"Let me know when you want me to take over...I don't want you to hurt yourself."

"Okay, but I can handle it," I managed to say between grunts, struggling to work the bike back down on my own. I very carefully backed up, this time leaning into the mountain so I wouldn't tumble downhill. With stubborn determination, I continued up the steepest, most difficult terrain I'd ever attempted on a motorcycle. About halfway up, my front tire hit yet another rock just at the right angle and flipped me around again. My heart was pounding; my breath was short and fast. I looked down below at William, his arms crossed over the handlebars and looking very concerned.

"Okay," I said meekly. "I think I'll let you take over."

We switched vehicles and he rode the dirt bike up to

the area where it was smooth again. I followed along on the four-wheeler, but even that was hard to control on this terrain. At the top, we switched again and continued on our journey through the mountains and valleys of Colorado.

I would not have traded that experience for anything, especially after God later revealed to me a greater lesson about my awesome journey up the mountain.

About three months after that experience, I awoke in the middle of the night—which wasn't surprising because I do a lot of praying in the early hours. The moment I opened my eyes, I knew the Lord was relaying something to me, and I did not want to miss the message. I jumped out of bed and walked quickly to my office. Tears began to fill my eyes, and I grabbed a pen and paper. The thoughts were coming too fast, so I grabbed a digital voice recorder instead. The message was clear. God impressed on me something He wanted me to realize and to tell others.

Now, I've never heard God speak audibly (and if I did, I would probably run out of the house). But there was no mistaking what He wanted me to know. As I began speaking into the recorder, I was crying so hard it was hard for me to talk. I don't know why I was so emotional, but then again it's not every day the Lord speaks to me! In Galatians 1:11-12, Paul talks about receiving a revelation from Jesus Christ. I believe that is what I received as well. Paul writes, "I want you to know, brothers, that the gospel I preached is not something that man made up. I did not receive it from any man, nor was I taught it;

rather, I received it by revelation from Jesus Christ."

The message I felt God impressing on my heart was related to my motorcycle ride. He pointed out to me a parallel between that experience and my relationship with Him. You know the story—I rode up that rough, rocky road determined that "I" could do it. William kept asking, "You want me to take it from here? Do you need any help? You want me to take over?" My stubborn answer was always, "No, I got it. I can do it." I refused help from the expert, and he waited and watched patiently while I almost killed myself trying to get through it alone.

My revelation from all of this? We all struggle through rough and rocky roads in our lives. Through it all, God is there: watching to see if we'll call on Him. He is just waiting for us to surrender and say, "Okay, God. I can't do this anymore. I need your help." And that's when He comes in and helps us! For so many years, I've tried to "fix" problems or do things on my own. Often, it's only when I'm at my wits end that I call on God for help. I should be calling on God first, not last!

Psalm 50:15 says, "And call on me in the day of trouble; I will deliver you, and you will honor me." God tells us to call on Him when we are in trouble. That doesn't mean your problem will be solved immediately (although it might be), but it means He will be with you while you are going through your trial. Trust me; you want God with you and on your side when you're going through a rocky time in life. He is the *only one* who can give you peace in the middle of a trial. Don't wait to call on God or use Him as the last resort. He should be first and foremost in your thoughts and priorities because He is there for you.

Take advantage of our God, who loves us and cares for us. Make it a habit to call on Him first, not when all else fails.

Let me ask you something. Have you put your faith in Him? He died for you. If you have not put your faith in Him, I want you to stop right now, be still, and say this prayer:

"Today, I'm putting my faith in You, the One who died for me. I'm trusting You, and I want a relationship with You." First Peter 5:7 says, "Cast all your anxiety on him because he cares for you." It's not during the good times that our faith grows; it's during the trials. We have access to Him, so we can turn over our troubles to Him. When you see how He handles situations, your faith will grow, and you will trust Him more and more. I know Him more intimately in the middle of my trials, because I'm aware that He sustains me during them.

> The message was clear. God impressed on me something He wanted me to realize and to tell others.

He supplies the all-surpassing peace that the Bible says we can't even begin to understand. We reaffirm our faith (to Him and others) whenever we leave it in His hands. Faith is trusting Him.

Of course, you might have to keep reaffirming your faith because we tend to take it back and "do it ourselves." We all go through difficult times in our lives, and sometimes we think we can "fix things" on our own. I believe God allows things to happen in our lives to bring us closer to Him. You don't develop a closer relationship when everything is going great; it's when you are in the trenches that you call out to God and say, "Okay God, I can't do this on my own! I need Your help, Your guidance, Your peace, Your direction, Your strength, Your encouragement. Help me!" And that's when He takes over.

But you must let Him have it and not keep stepping in and trying to take it back. He is in control; let Him guide and help you in each decision you need to make. This has happened many times in my life, and I'm finally "getting it" after 40 years! Let God be God. I promise, you will be so much better off not trying to "do it yourself!" Like being on a dirt bike trying to get up the side of Aspen Mountain, we can't always see what's ahead; we must put all our faith in the One who knows what's around the corner!

NAY, NAY ‒ STAY AWAY FROM STRANGERS

WHEN I WAS FIVE YEARS OLD, MY PARENTS DECIDED to move our family to an area of Dallas called Highland Park, a nice area with huge trees and beautiful homes. They chose that area because it has good schools, the neighborhood is safe, and it is full of young families and kids. We lived just four blocks from Bradfield Elementary where I went to school. That's when I met my friend, Cynthia Love, in the first grade. When we reached the second grade, our parents let us walk home from school together since we lived just one block apart.

One day at school, we watched a short film about

staying away from strangers. The reel-to-reel film had a cute little cartoon donkey that warned children, "Nay, nay! Stay away from strangers!" Then he would kick at a cartoon "stranger" to prove his point. As Cynthia and I walked home that very day, two boys (ones I happened to have a crush on) started teasing us and throwing things at us. I walked across the street by myself to get away from them, and Cynthia walked on ahead. She thought I was with the boys, but I was walking alone down a street called Lomo Alto.

Suddenly, I heard a man whisper, "Pssst! Pssst!" I stopped and looked over my right shoulder. I saw a man crouched down in someone's backyard in the bushes. He was wearing a tan corduroy jacket and had sandy, brown hair down to his shoulders. He motioned me closer to him, but there was a chain-link fence between us, covered with thick bushes.

He said, "Hey, do you know what time it is?" I panicked, knowing something was wrong.

"No..." I said quietly, frozen in place.

"Can you help me find my little kitty?" he asked next.

"Um...I can't," I said quickly. "I have a ballet lesson." I was lying; I didn't have ballet, but I was feeling even more anxious at this point.

"It will just take a couple of minutes. I need to find her."

I looked down the street. Cynthia was out of yelling distance, but I could still see her.

"Well, okay," I agreed hesitantly, "but my mom is waiting for me."

I walked into the backyard toward the woodpile.

My arms were full of books, and I was wearing my favorite blue fur.

"Here, kitty kitty kitty," he called. "Hey, let's see if she is in the garage."

The door was rolled up and when I looked inside the garage, there was only a sofa and chair. He said, "Maybe she's on top of the garage door. Why don't you get on my shoulders and see if you can see her?"

"Okay," I agreed, setting my blue fur coat on top of my books near the entrance of the garage. As he helped me up on his shoulders, I suddenly heard a loud, distinct "meow."

"Did you hear that?" he said and walked over closer to the garage door.

"Yes, I did!" I said and peered around, trying to see the cat.

"I can't see anything," I concluded. "I'm not tall enough."

"I have an idea," he suggested. "Why don't you get down, and we will slowly shut the garage door. That way, if she is up there, she can jump down."

I knew as he pulled down the garage door something bad was about to happen. Even as a second-grader, my intuition told me I was not in a good place. I was right—I was not in a good place at all. After he shut the door, it got real dark, real quickly. There was a window in the back of the garage near the sofa and chair, and I could see a neighbor watering his grass two doors down. I was hoping he would somehow see me inside.

Then the man pulled his pants down and said, "Come over here."

I did, but I turned away and continued to watch the neighbor watering his lawn. The stranger was now sitting in the chair beside the sofa. I was so frightened I started praying out loud, "Dear God, please let me go home. God, I want to go home." As my prayers grew louder and louder, he said, "Okay, okay! Shhh! Be quiet. I'll let you go." I ran to my books and gathered up my coat saying, "God! God, help me!"

The man opened the garage door just enough for me to get out. I ran all the way home and through the back alley that I knew so well. Nobody could catch me there.

I popped out of the alley and ran into our driveway. By now, I was crying and very upset. Mom was backing her 1970 yellow and black Pontiac out of our garage. I still remember her expression when she looked at me in total confusion. She threw the car

One day at school, we watched a short film about staying away from strangers.

into "park," got out, and wrapped her arms around my blue fur and me. "A man tried to get me," I sobbed.

For the next several weeks, I looked through hundreds of mug shots trying to identify the man. They never caught him. Not many people know this story, only a few close friends. The reason I am telling you this is because I want to stress how important it is to tell children at a very young age about God and Jesus. Maybe God allowed this to happen to me so I could pass this story along to you, 40 years later.

My parents taught me that God was always there for me. Even though I couldn't see Him, He was with me and He loved me no matter what I did. We talked about God and Jesus in our home, at the dinner table, and at night. Each evening, Dad gathered the family together to read family devotionals and pray together before we went to sleep. God was with us everywhere we went. Even at the age of eight, I knew to call on God in the day of trouble. I knew the moment I began calling out to God that He would answer me and protect me from what that man was probably planning to do. God intervened in a huge way for me that day.

When you call out His name, He is there, and He is with you. Not only have I experienced that truth; He confirms it in the Bible. A verse I refer to often is Psalm 50:15: "Call upon me in the day of trouble; I will deliver you, and you will honor me." And Psalm 46:1 says, "God is our refuge (a place of security) and strength, an ever-present help in trouble" (parentheses added). The next verse in that chapter says, "Therefore we will not fear..."

I can't imagine not having God in my life. He is our refuge and strength—He's always there for us and we need not be afraid. If you don't have God in your life, what do you have? You have yourself; you're alone. When you surrender to God and ask Him into your life, you will never be alone. God is always with you.

When God Intervenes in
SCRIPTURE

GOD'S WORD IS FOR YOUR GOOD

IT'S SO IMPORTANT TO BE FIRMLY PLANTED IN GOD'S Word! The Bible says, "All scripture is given by inspiration of God, and is profitable for doctrine, for reproof, for correction, for instruction in righteousness, that the man of God may be complete, thoroughly equipped for every good work" 2 Timothy 3:16-17, NKJ. That means all of Scripture is for our good— His promises *and* His commands. I hope this book encourages you to read more of God's Word. I'll get you started with a list of some of my favorite verses below. Read them for yourself, and commit them to memory.

Exodus 14:14 "The Lord will fight for you, you need only to be still."

2 Chronicles 20:15 "...do not be afraid or discouraged...For the battle is not yours, but God's."

Psalm 31:14 "But I trust in you, O Lord; I say, 'You are my God; my times are in your hands.'"

Psalm 46:1 "God is our refuge and strength, an ever-present help in trouble."

*Isaiah 43:2 "When you pass through the waters,
I will be with you; and when you pass through the
rivers, they will not sweep over you.
When you walk through the fire, you will not be
burned; the flames will not set you ablaze."*

*Psalm 57:1 "Have mercy on me, O God, have mercy
on me, for in you my soul takes refuge.
I will take refuge in the shadow of your wings until
the disaster has passed."*

*Psalm 50:15 "And call upon me in the day of trouble; I
will deliver you, and you will honor me."*

*Psalm 61:1-3 "Hear my cry, O God; listen to my
prayer. From the ends of the earth I call to you, I call
as my heart grows faint; lead me to the rock that is
higher than I. For you have been my refuge, a strong
tower against the foe."*

*Psalm 62:5 "Find rest, O my soul, in God alone; my
hope comes from him. He alone is my rock and my
salvation; he is my fortress, I will not be shaken."*

*Isaiah 58:9 "Then you will call, and the Lord will answer;
you will cry for help, and he will say: Here am I."*

*John 6:47 "I tell you the truth, he who believes has
everlasting life."*

John 8:47 "He who belongs to God hears what God says. The reason you do not hear is that you do not belong to God."

John 11:25-26 "Jesus said to her, 'I am the resurrection and the life. He who believes in me will live, even though he dies; and whoever lives and believes in me will never die. Do you believe this?'"

John 14:6 "Jesus answered, 'I am the way and the truth and the life. No one comes to the Father except through me.'"

Acts 4:12 "Salvation is found in no one else, for there is no other name under heaven given to men by which we must be saved."

Romans 1:4 "...and who through the Spirit of holiness was declared with power to be the Son of God by his resurrection from the dead: Jesus Christ our Lord."

Romans 1:20 "For since the creation of the world God's invisible qualities—his eternal power and divine nature—have been clearly seen, being understood from what has been made, so that men are without excuse."

Romans 5:1-8 "Therefore, since we have been justified through faith, we have peace with God through our Lord Jesus Christ, through whom we have gained access by faith into this grace in which we now stand. And we rejoice in the hope of the glory of God. Not

*only so, but we also rejoice in our sufferings, because
we know that suffering produces perseverance;
perseverance, character; and character, hope. And
hope does not disappoint us, because God has poured
out his love into our hearts by the Holy Spirit, whom
he has given us. You see, at just the right time, when
we were still powerless, Christ died for the ungodly.
Very rarely will anyone die for a righteous man,
though for a good man someone might possibly dare to
die. But God demonstrates his own love for us in this:
While we were still sinners, Christ died for us."*

*Romans 6:23 "For the wages of sin is death, but the
gift of God is eternal life in Christ Jesus our Lord."*

*Ephesians 2:8-9 "For it is by grace you have been
saved, through faith—and this not from yourselves, it is
the gift of God—not by works, so that no one can boast."*

*Ephesians 3:20 "Now to him who is able to do
immeasurably more than all we ask or imagine,
according to his power that is at work within us, to him
be glory in the church and in Christ Jesus throughout
all generations, for ever and ever! Amen."*

*Ephesians 4:5 "...one Lord, one faith, one baptism;
one God and Father of all, who is over all and through
all and in all."*

*1 Peter 5:7 "Cast all your anxiety on him,
because he cares for you."*

1 Peter 5:10-11 "And the God of all grace, who called you to his eternal glory in Christ, after you have suffered a little while, will himself restore you and make you strong, firm and steadfast. To him be the power forever and ever."

Revelation 21:4 "He will wipe every tear from their eyes. There will be no more death or mourning or crying or pain, for the old order of things has passed away."

WALKING WHERE JESUS WALKED

I'VE HAD THE OPPORTUNITY TO GO TO ISRAEL AND GREECE twice, and these trips had a tremendous impact on me. In March 2010, I was fortunate to take my niece, Adrienne, on her first trip to Israel. It was one of the most memorable times in my life to spend 10 days with her. I couldn't get enough of the history and the sites where the stories from the Bible actually took place. Even today when I read the Bible, I'm able to picture where those events occurred. For example, I've seen the pool of Bethesda where Jesus healed the lame man. It's a beautiful area in Jerusalem, with tall, stone arches and pathways around pools that used to hold water. The story is told in John 5:1-15:

Some time later, Jesus went up to Jerusalem for a feast

of the Jews. Now there is in Jerusalem near the Sheep Gate a pool, which in Aramaic is called Bethesda and which is surrounded by five covered colonnades. Here a great number of disabled people used to lay—the blind, the lame, the paralyzed. One who was there had been an invalid for thirty-eight years. When Jesus saw him lying there and learned that he had been in this condition for a long time, he asked him, "Do you want to get well?"

"Sir," the invalid replied, "I have no one to help me into the pool when the water is stirred. While I am trying to get in, someone else goes down ahead of me."

Then Jesus said to him, "Get up! Pick up your mat and walk." At once the man was cured; he picked up his mat and walked. The day on which this took place was a Sabbath, and so the Jews said to the man who had been healed, "It is the Sabbath; the law forbids you to carry your mat."

But he replied, "The man who made me well said to me, 'Pick up your mat and walk.' "

So they asked him, "Who is this fellow who told you to pick it up and walk?"

The man who was healed had no idea who it was, for Jesus had slipped away into the crowd that was there.

Later Jesus found him at the temple and said to him, "See, you are well again. Stop sinning or something worse may happen to you." The man went away and told the Jews that it was Jesus who had made him well.

We also visited the Mount of Beatitudes, where Jesus gave the Sermon on the Mount in

Matthew 5, one of His greatest speeches recorded in the Bible. It overlooks the Sea of Galilee, which is actually a big lake (13 miles long, 7 miles wide). It is a beautiful setting up on a hill. As our guide, Dr. Bill Counts, read from the Bible about what took place there, I could look across the fields full of mustard seed flowers and visualize Jesus standing down below. I could picture the hillsides packed with thousands of people anxious to hear what He had to say.

Matthew 5:3-12 says:

Blessed are the poor in spirit,
for theirs is the kingdom of heaven.
Blessed are those who mourn,
for they will be comforted.
Blessed are the meek, for they will inherit the earth.
Blessed are those who hunger and thirst for
righteousness, for they will be filled.
Blessed are the merciful, for they will be shown mercy.
Blessed are the pure in heart, for they will see God.
Blessed are the peacemakers,
for they will be called sons of God.
Blessed are those who are persecuted because of
righteousness, for theirs is the kingdom of heaven.
Blessed are you when people insult you, persecute you,
and falsely say all kinds of evil against you because of
me. Rejoice and be glad, because great is your reward
in heaven, for in the same way they persecuted the
prophets who were before you.

The gardens at the Mount of Beatitudes are beautifully landscaped and have gorgeous two-color roses among many other flowers to enjoy. There are several benches underneath the huge trees that cover the hilltop—a very serene, peaceful, and special place. It was so neat to be there with Little A and see everything through her eyes. I especially enjoyed praying and reading the Bible together in this setting. Praying for her at the Wailing Wall was something we will never forget.

We stayed at a hotel on the Sea of Galilee for two nights. Each morning, I woke up early and full of excitement for the day ahead. I sipped a cup of coffee on my balcony overlooking the lake as the sun came up over the mountains for a beautiful sunrise. Some wooden boats, replicas of the ones back in Jesus' day, quietly sailed through the reflection of the sun off the water. So peaceful. I read from the gospels (Matthew, Mark, Luke, and John) about what Jesus did and where He lived in that particular area.

The second day, we took a boat ride on one of those very boats I'd seen on the water. There were 52 of us from Texas on the boat; it was quite a sight! The ship's crew raised the American flag, and we put our hands on our hearts to sing our national anthem. We also sang several worship songs. Dr. Counts once again read the scriptures that described this beautiful place. He helped us realize we were literally walking in Jesus' footsteps on this trip.

Dr. Counts said, "In Israel, it's possible to know the area (and sometimes very close to the exact spot) where certain biblical events happened or where Jesus walked, spoke, or performed miracles." Then he looked around over the water and added, "We know for certain that the place where we are right now on the Sea of Galilee is the same lake and the same view that Jesus had every day. This is the same lake where He walked on water. These are the very seashores He walked along. And this is the very place where the crowds followed Him, and He spoke to them."

Because the lake is 680 feet below sea level, storms can brew quickly over the mountains without warning. Matthew 8:23-27 tells us about a storm that surprised the disciples on the Sea of Galilee:

Then he got into the boat and his disciples followed him. Without warning, a furious storm came up on the lake, so that the waves swept over the boat. But Jesus was sleeping. The disciples went and woke him, saying, "Lord, save us! We're going to drown!" He replied, "You of little faith, why are you so afraid?" Then he got up and rebuked the winds and the waves, and it was completely calm. The men were amazed and asked, "What kind of man is this? Even the winds and the waves obey him!"

> The second day, we took a boat ride on one of those very boats I'd seen on the water.

I know this is a true story because God rebuked the flames that almost engulfed our house in Santa Barbara. He can calm a storm or hold back a 200-foot wall of flames!

Another one of the most memorable stories in the Bible was when Jesus walked on the water. Once again, He was on the Sea of Galilee! Matthew 14:22-32 tells the story:

Immediately Jesus made the disciples get into the boat and go on ahead of him to the other side, while he dismissed the crowd. After he had dismissed them, he went up on a mountainside by himself to pray. When evening came, he was there alone, but the boat was already a considerable distance from land, buffeted by the waves because the wind was against it.

During the fourth watch of the night Jesus went out to them, walking on the lake. When the disciples saw him walking on the lake, they were terrified. "It's a ghost," they said, and cried out in fear.

But Jesus immediately said to them: "Take courage! It is I. Don't be afraid."

"Lord, if it's you," Peter replied, "tell me to come to you on the water."

"Come," he said.

Then Peter got down out of the boat, walked on the water and came toward Jesus. But when he saw the wind, he was afraid and, beginning to sink, cried out, "Lord, save me!"

Immediately Jesus reached out his hand and caught him. "You of little faith," he said, "why did you doubt?"

And when they climbed into the boat, the wind died down. Then those who were in the boat worshiped him, saying, "Truly you are the Son of God."

What an incredible experience to have seen Jesus walking on water, and because of his faith, Peter got out of the boat and went to Jesus. That story is a great reminder to us to "get out of the boat" and go to Jesus in faith, knowing He will be there for us. We must have the faith to step out of the boat, even when we are not sure what is going to happen. We can trust God, no matter the outcome, and have faith that His plans are best—no matter what. The Bible tells us these stories so we can learn by example and take these lessons to heart.

As I look back at my stories in this book, I guess you could say I "got out of the boat" a few times. I left my comfort zone and kept my eyes on Jesus. Did you notice that when Peter took his eyes off Jesus he began to sink? Has that ever happened to you? If you take your focus off Jesus, you begin to sink in despair and things fall apart around you. Keep your eyes on Jesus.

My faith and trust in the Lord allowed me to step out into the unknown and completely depend on the Lord. No matter what my circumstances, the Lord is faithful, and I will forever trust Him with my life. Jesus and I have a pact now. I completely trust and believe in Him for everything, and He takes care of my needs. He gives me the peace that surpasses all understanding, especially in the middle of my trials. It is a relief to know that He is in control, not me!

Remember the story of David and Goliath? We also went to the Valley of Elah where their battle took place. It's a beautiful valley, and it probably looks exactly as it did thousands of years ago, with flowers riddled between the same tall, green grass blowing in the wind. We walked to the riverbed where David gathered his five stones. Our guide, "Shmulik,"

read the story of David and Goliath from 1 Samuel 17 as we stood there. Smulik pointed out where the Israelites assembled their camp and the hill where the Philistines were living. We were standing between the two camps, next to the riverbed that divided the valley. As I listened to the story, I looked around me and visualized David, a "ruddy and handsome" sheepherder going up against Goliath, a nine-foot giant with a shield and sword, covered head to toe in bronze armor. David approached the giant with only his shepherd's staff, five smooth stones, and a slingshot. However, with the first throw, he hit Goliath in the forehead (the one area not covered by his helmet) and that giant dropped like a shot cow. First Samuel 17:46-47 tells us what David said to Goliath right before he killed him:

"This day the Lord will hand you over to me, and I'll strike you down and cut off your head. Today I will give the carcasses of the Philistine army to the birds of the air and the beasts of the earth, and the whole world will know that there is a God in Israel. All those gathered here will know that it is not by sword or spear that the Lord saves; for the battle is the Lord's, and he will give all of you into our hands."

I don't know about you, but David sounds to me like a man with a strong faith in God! He, too, sends us a great message about trusting in God. Before the battle even started, he boldly declared to his enemy that the Lord would defeat him. Your enemy today is likely not a physical giant like Goliath, but it might be a financial struggle, or a problem in your marriage, or any number of things. The point is that the battle is the Lord's. Trust Him to provide and protect you. And when He gets you through the battles in your life, give him the credit just as David did. Honor God and give Him the glory. It's not what *you* have done or an enemy *you* have defeated; it's what God does *through you*, because you believe.

Of course the Garden of Gethsemane was another incredible sight in Israel. A large garden area filled with old, beautiful olive trees marks the spot where Jesus prayed on the night before He was crucified. It is enclosed by an ancient stone wall and is located just outside the Temple walls and the Old City. Just hours before He was betrayed and arrested, Mark 14:35 tells us Jesus "fell to the ground and prayed that if possible the hour might pass from him." Jesus prayed, "Abba, Father, everything is possible for you. Take this cup from me. Yet not what I will, but what you will."

> I don't know about you, but David sounds to me like a man with a strong faith in God!

Jesus knew the terrible suffering He was about to endure, yet He prayed for God's will and not His own. He then endured torture far beyond what our minds can comprehend. Why? Because it was His Father's will for Him to die on the cross for our sins. Because Jesus obeyed, we now have the opportunity to receive eternal life. It's a gift. You don't have to earn it. You've been saved through your faith in Jesus; it's not what you do in life that saves you. It is a gift of God—not by your own good deeds, so that no one can brag about it (Ephesians 2:8-9). All you have to do to receive this gift is believe in Jesus. Believe He died for you, He rose three days later, and now He lives in heaven with God the Father.

Many people think they are not "righteous" enough to go to heaven; they fear being "judged" by God. One day, you will stand before the Judge (God) in heaven, and He will ask you one question: "Why didn't you follow Me? You decided to live in sin and shame and do whatever you wanted to do."

You will not have a lawyer with you to defend you when you stand in front of the Judge—it will be only you and Him. However, if you believe in Jesus Christ and have asked Him into your heart and life, things will be very different on that day. You will no longer be standing in front of a Judge—you will be standing before your heavenly Father. Jesus Himself will be standing there with you, and the Father will then say: "I know this one. This one is mine."

What is keeping you from trusting Him right now? Jesus is the one who can set you free from your bondage, guilt, and shame. He died for you so you could be free from all that. What a relief! If you're ready to commit yourself to Christ, ask God silently or aloud (right now!):

"Lord, please come into my life. Open my heart and my eyes to see You and know that You are here for me. I believe You died on the cross for my sins. Because of that fact, I can live my life knowing I am one of Your

children. I know You will always love and care for me. I acknowledge that I am a sinner, and I need Your help. I desire to be in Your will and to follow You. Thank You, Lord, for dying on the cross for me. I praise You and honor You in all that I do. Amen."

That's a pretty detailed prayer, but a simple, "Lord, I ask You to come into my heart," is all you need if you truly believe in Him.

On the other hand, if you are not ready to pray that prayer because you are having a hard time believing in Christ, ask Him to reveal Himself to you. Ask God to open your eyes and your heart to see Him clearly and not be distracted by Satan, the world, or anything or anyone else that would pull you away from the truth. God is real, and He is waiting for you to come and rest in Him.

I've had people ask me, "Why did God send His Son to earth to die for us?" First of all, I don't question why God does things. I trust that He knows best, and He knows the outcome of what He is doing in our lives and in the world.

Still, most people want to know why God does the things He does. Well, I do too! I just believe everything happens for a reason. I might not understand His ways, His purpose, or His reason. I simply trust and have faith in Him. As the title of this book suggests, He has intervened and shown me many times that He is in control. He can handle everything. It's not up to me to try and figure out "why." It's up to me to obey and trust Him. God is so beyond our intelligence; we cannot wrap our minds around Him. Therefore, He sent Jesus, in human form, so we could grasp a little bit of how magnificent He truly is.

I'm not one to insist on seeing "the facts." I simply believe in God because I believe the Bible and what it tells us. Even when Moses asked God to show him His glory, God refused. He said:

"I will cause all my goodness to pass in front of you, and I will proclaim my name, the Lord, in your presence. I will have mercy on whom I will have mercy, and I will have compassion on whom I will have compassion. But," he said, "you cannot see my face, for no one may see me and live." Then the Lord said, "There is a place near me where you may stand on a rock. When my glory passes by, I will put you in a cleft in the rock and cover you with my hand until I have passed by. Then I will remove my hand and you will see my back; but my face must not be seen." Exodus 33:19-23

To see God's "back" means we can only see where God has been. I've seen where God has been and what He has done in my life. I don't have to see His face, because I see *where He has been.*

A SPECIAL NOTE TO MY READERS: FROM MY HEART TO YOURS

As the chapters of our lives unfold, so do the opportunities for God to intervene, and I always say…Let Him! The last two years of my life have been a struggle in more ways than one, but never did I sway in my faith. If anything, these trials I endure have brought me closer to the Lord in more ways than I could imagine. I fought the good fight and stuck with what I believe because *When God Has A Way, No Other Way Works.*

Some of you may realize I changed my name—to me, it represents a new beginning in my life. I look forward with great anticipation to see what God has planned for my future. I'm starting fresh and moving on with my life. He once again has brought me peace and comfort through these difficult times.

Just because I have written a book about "God" does not mean I escape hardships and calamity. We will all face trials and tribulations throughout our lives, but if you have God in your heart, and life, He will intervene and give you the peace and strength to sustain you during your trial.

Even today, I thank the Lord for each trial He has set before me. We learn to depend and trust Him during difficulty more so than at any other time. If you find it hard to put your trust in Christ, ask Him to reveal Himself to you. I have chosen to put my trust in Him, and I challenge you to do the same.

Remember, *When God Intervenes, Let Him!*